THEY MADE YOU BOSS
— NOW WHAT?

PETER WOAN

THEY MADE YOU BOSS

— NOW WHAT?

59 Things You Need to Know

To order additional copies of this book, contact:
Xlibris Corporation
1-888-795-4274
www.Xlibris.com
Orders@Xlibris.com
20178

CONTENTS

To Rebecca

ACKNOWLEDGEMENTS

For their constructive criticisms and insightful suggestions, I would like to thank Penny Ritchie-Calder, Sarah Ritchie-Calder, Michael Sherley-Dale, Cheryl McPhilimy of McPhilimy Associates in Chicago, and my wife, Rebecca Woan.

INTRODUCTION

There is no shortage of bad bosses in corporate America, but it does not have to be that way. Although some people might have a greater aptitude to be leaders than followers, being a good boss is an acquired skill. Unfortunately, it is a skill that few new bosses are being taught. American companies are relatively good at teaching the functional skills of management, such as how to make presentations, how to conduct performance reviews, how to prepare a budget. They are not so good at telling their new managers how to handle those everyday events, ranging from the humdrum to the critical, that comprise a boss's typical working day. In other words, they don't prepare people to be a boss.

Instead, this learning experience becomes one of trial and error that is debilitating for both the new boss and the employees. It's bad enough that most managers are given the job and pushed out to do it largely unaided, but they then have to practice their skills on real people whose careers and daily sense of well-being depend so much on the person they report to.

For corporate employees, having a bad boss changes everything. Even when it's going well, work can be a stressful place, and it's where employees spend much of their adult waking life. If people are unhappy at work, it will affect everything they do, and unhappiness at work is often the result of having a bad boss.

There is little need to write a book about how a manager should cope when things are going well. This means most of the following chapters deal with the challenges and difficulties of being a manager, and so the result is a book that might be seen as pessimistic. This is not the intended message. First, bear in mind that even though you may read about successive problematic issues, they will not come at you quite so relentlessly in the workplace. In between the managerial challenges are periods of relative calm. Leading a group of committed professionals in a successful enterprise that meets its goals and provides job satisfaction can be an exhilarating experience and well worth having to deal with any negatives.

The book contains fifty-nine chapters, each discussing a different aspect of what it's like to be the boss. With a few exceptions, the chapters are short. Just as the topics in the book are not over analyzed, neither should the manager spend too much time pondering individual issues: there are just too many things going on that need attention.

Note on the use of the word "boss"

In the workplace, the word "boss" has mixed meanings, not all complimentary. Because of this, people tend to use other less emotive words like "supervisor," as well of course "manager." Interestingly, you seldom hear people refer to the boss as their "leader," unless in an ironic context such as "Our fearless leader." In the book, I use "boss" with no negative undertones, simply as a way of identifying the person to whom others report. Rather than use the awkward "he or she" when referring to the boss, I alternate between the two at random.

1

THEY MADE YOU BOSS

Your first reaction—and that of others

You've just been given the good news: You've been promoted and are now a boss.

It is an achievement of which you should rightly feel proud. In corporate America, it is still the clearest public sign of success. These are some of the thoughts that may pass through your mind: My talent for leadership has been recognized; my hard work has been appreciated; it is the first step up the corporate ladder; will I get more money and some new perks? In addition, you will almost certainly feel a greater sense of loyalty to your company than you had before.

These are all normal feelings, but even at this early stage you should understand that the attitude of the people who promoted you might be more ambiguous. These feelings might include: There was no one else suitable and it was too expensive to hire someone from outside; we could have done worse, let's hope he doesn't mess things up too badly; hopefully the thrill of promotion will substitute for not paying him more money till next year.

This is an exaggerated perspective; even if there are some misgivings about your promotion, there will almost certainly be plenty of genuine goodwill and hope, because almost everyone has an interest in the new boss succeeding rather than failing.

The point of this first chapter is to remind you right from the start that there will be many different perspectives on your promotion, as there are on every aspect of work in corporate America. Perhaps the most important perspectives will come from the people who will be reporting to you. Some of them will be veterans of management changes, many of them will be career employees who may never get put in a supervisory role, and few if any will share your own personal excitement at your promotion.

For many of them, their response will be initial apprehension, along with a belief that it's the same old corporate song, just with a different singer. Your challenge, among other things, is to show them how things will be different and better, to win their respect but not necessarily their affection, and to extract from them their best work. Remember that if you are a new boss, all your past success has been because of what you personally accomplished. Any future success now depends almost entirely on how well other people perform. That is a huge difference.

2

ANDY WARHOL

In the future everyone will be famous for fifteen minutes.
—ANDY WARHOL

Start by giving everyone some individual attention

This chapter is about giving everyone within your responsibility their "fifteen minutes" as soon as possible after you have taken over. This means announcing that you are going to meet privately with every member of the department or unit within the next few weeks to hear how they view their jobs, what they like and don't like, any ideas they may have on procedures, ideas on productivity, ideas on almost anything as long as it is related to the job. You should do this even if you have been promoted from within the operation you are now managing, and already know everyone.

In some respects, it is an amnesty, where they have a chance to be critical with the tacit understanding that any criticisms they make are of the former leadership rather than yours. This is important, because as time passes, their world becomes less of what you inherited and more of what you are making it. Unless you meet them alone and quickly, you lose this window, and they will become less willing to talk frankly. Whatever they may say about your predecessor, it is important that you not criticize him.

These sessions are good for you because you should know how they feel about themselves and their jobs, how they feel about the operation and to a lesser extent about their colleagues. Some of what you hear might shock you, especially if it is coming from people who you worked with and thought you knew.

Listen a lot more than you talk. Prompt them with "open" questions such as, "What do you like best about what you do?" Don't ask "closed" questions (ones that can be answered yes, no or in one word) such as the particularly unhelpful, "Are you happy here?"

It's good for the staff too. Outside of the annual review process, it is unlikely that they will have had this chance before. You might be surprised how appreciative people are at being given this chance to talk; in the work place everyone wants their voice to be heard to some degree. They will like the fact that you did not simply take over and assume you knew how they felt either by rumor, or by merely looking at their personal files (which you should always do anyway).

What if you are following a boss who was well respected and who will be missed? The things that made her popular will probably emerge during these meetings. While you should pay attention, the focus of the discussion should be the person herself. However good the former boss might have been, it is unlikely he made everyone equally contented. If the operation is in good shape, not derailing it can be a challenge. There is always room for innovation and improvement, but if things are going well you should probably make any changes carefully.

Another suggestion for these private sessions: try to avoid exclaiming, "What a great idea! We'll get that changed immediately!" because, as we'll see in Chapter 14, everything you say will be remembered. And each day that goes by without you taking care of it, disillusion and resentment grows—fairly or not.

It's also a way for the staff to get a good look at you, and therefore a chance for you to present yourself in as favorable a light as you can. However tough and uncompromising you might have to be in the future, they will at least know you have the capacity to be somewhat sympathetic and thoughtful.

3

KING LEAR

Don't avoid reality, embrace it

It's been said that a lack of reality is the perquisite of two groups of people: the young and those in positions of authority. As far as the young are concerned, it is understandable: they just haven't been around long enough to know how things really are. But for those in authority, it's a very different dynamic. They can be cut off from reality for two reasons, first because the people who report to them are reluctant to pass on bad news, and second because those same people tend to agree with whatever the boss says, however ridiculous it may be.

It's not surprising: few people want to be the deliverer of bad news to a boss who is liable to punish the messenger or always associate him with negativity. And how often can you really expect to disagree with the boss before she gets weary of it? "Hey," she starts to think, "if you're so smart and I'm so dumb, why am I the boss and you're not?" The result is that the boss becomes insulated from bad news while at the same time developing an exaggerated sense of her own competence. Everything she says will usually find at least one person eager to endorse it as brilliant.

This resulting lack of reality can become the norm rather than the exception. Your challenge as a boss is to guard against it.

You must be prepared to hear things you don't want to; it's not easy. Look at what happened to Cordelia in Shakespeare's *King Lear*. He wanted his daughters to tell him in extravagant language how much they loved him. The first two daughters did, but Cordelia refused to oblige her father and was banished from the kingdom for not telling him what he wanted to hear. No one likes hearing bad news or having to face an unpleasant reality, but don't be like King Lear: Confront it.

One important way you can help maintain a grip on reality is to work at being approachable. Being a good listener is always respected—it's rare—as most people are anxious for their voice to be heard rather than to hear someone else's. However just being willing to listen is not enough. You have to be seen by your staff to respond to what you hear. Listening and then ignoring is the almost the same as not listening.

It takes most managers some time—often years—before they realize the value of informed outside input. Some managers never understand it. The difficulty for new managers is that they feel being influenced by the opinion of others is an early sign of weakness. Of course, if the new manager avoids decisions by always clinging to the advice of others, this might be true; the skill is to appear in control while at the same time receptive to any good ideas. If this is achieved, the move to seek input will be seen as a strength, not a weakness. Last, and not insignificantly, by listening to others you will get some very good ideas.

4

GREAT EXPECTATIONS

Tell people clearly what you expect from them

People at work have to know what is expected of them. There are many things that bosses and companies can require of their employees, but whatever is required has to be conveyed clearly to the staff. You can't keep your expectations secret and hope that people will read your mind.

This is harder to do than it sounds, because as the boss, probably possessed of some vision and intelligence, you have a good idea of what needs to be done, and how it needs to be done. You might assume your employees implicitly understand this—it's clear enough to you. Well, some might but many will not, and so you must articulate these expectations so there is no misunderstanding.

Otherwise intelligent and thoughtful people often fail to appreciate how critical this is. Consequently, when the employees do not perform as the boss would like, the boss gets upset, but because she has not explicitly described what she wants, she finds it hard to correct. The typical result is a brooding boss, silently seething as employees continue to cause irritation without knowing why.

There are three broad aspects of expectations: (1) **what** you expect, (2) **how** you convey what you expect, and (3) **when** you convey what you expect.

First, what you expect. There are behavioral expectations such as work habits, dress codes, how people answer the phone, use of expense accounts. Then there are task-specific expectations that usually involve a more objective standard such as individual revenue goals.

How do you convey them? One way that should not be overlooked is the job description. Do the employees even have one? A new boss can use the job description on which to base her expectations. If there is no job description, she can begin to create one.

It is worth mentioning that for job descriptions, the amount of detail in the descriptions tends to increase as you move down the corporate ladder. For example, a description for the mailroom clerk has to be very specific: collect and deliver mail three times a day, collect and send outgoing faxes, collect and distribute incoming faxes and so on. In fact, the new boss should recognize that the lower down the salary scale you go, employees generally demand a more detailed job description. This is usually because (1) they need more direction, and (2) they don't especially want to be doing things they are not paid to do.

Usually the best time to outline expectations is at the employees' annual review. This is when the value of clear, written expectations really becomes apparent. It's very hard to conduct a meaningful performance appraisal if there are ambiguous benchmarks or no benchmarks.

However, it's a poor manager who saves everything up for a once-a-year discussion. Expectations therefore should also be announced and reiterated whenever appropriate throughout the year, to the staff collectively or to individuals.

I once read about a CEO who asked his top executives to write down the single biggest issue they thought the company faced. He was subsequently furious when most of them chose different things: some said labor issues, some said customer issues, and some said supplier issues. The "correct" answer—his answer— was the rising cost of their product. But the CEO was the one at fault. He should never have allowed his colleagues to be in a position where they did not all understand and agree on this point. He had wrongly assumed that his burning issue was everyone else's.

A leading cause of employee dissatisfaction is not knowing what is expected and therefore not knowing when either a good job or a bad job has been done. In the absence of a clear message, employees will have to rely on occasional words of praise or rebuke. Employees will be forced into interpreting the boss's demeanor and moods. Don't put your staff in this position: Tell them exactly what you expect, document it, remind them of it, and enforce it. And while you are on the subject, you should also tell them what you don't like!

5

EARLY INFLUENCES

The risk of being easily swayed

Many years ago, before going to college, a friend and I took a train to Istanbul from London, and then hitchhiked back. Apart from teaching me that in the future I should pay much closer attention to the scale of maps (it was a lot further than we thought), I learned a few other things.

When we were hitchhiking, we met many other hitchhikers, and hitchhikers like to talk about the places they have been on their travels. This usually took the form of an instant appraisal of a city or region, first in terms of how good the rides were and then any other notable features. Being relatively new to this world, we hung on the words of these seasoned travelers as they praised one city or vilified another. "Oh no," they'd say, "you don't want to go to _____," and we would take them at their word, even revising our route to avoid the unappealing place.

But, of course, it was illogical to base our decision on the subjective experience of one person. There were probably very specific reasons why someone had not enjoyed a certain city, and many thousands of other visitors probably had a great time there.

We had made the mistake of assigning too much importance to the comments of someone whom we viewed as being credible at a time when we were very susceptible to outside opinion. We were anxious for information about other places, but were not able to assess this information critically. Instead of noting an adverse comment as just one person's experience, we viewed it as the *correct* experience.

During the first few months after you become the boss, you will be extremely sensitive to information you think might help you learn your new role or give you some special insight. If someone has even a small amount of credibility, you will tend to attach undue weight to what they say.

This means that early on you could make some bad decisions or build up some unfounded prejudices based on one or two isolated comments. When you are starting off as the boss, it's hard not to be influenced by someone else's firm opinion expressed with confidence: Try not to be so easily and quickly impressed.

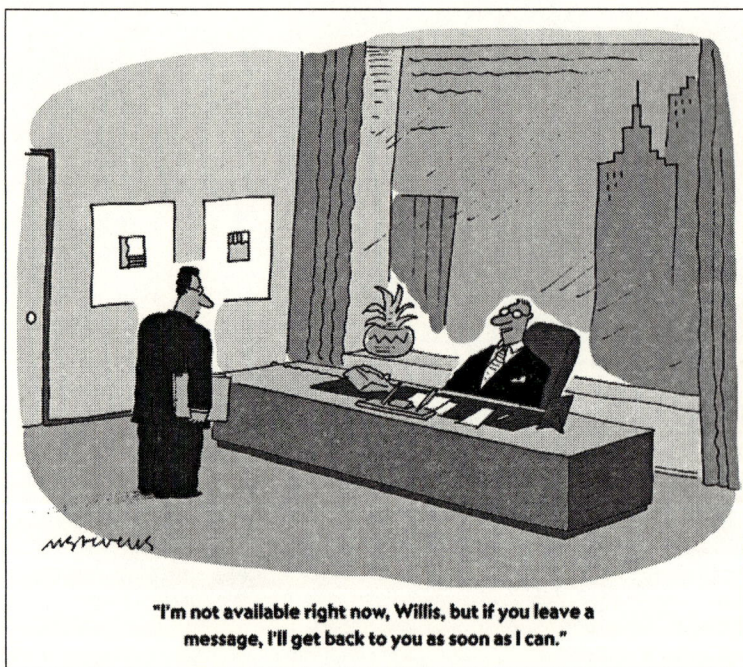

"I'm not available right now, Willis, but if you leave a message, I'll get back to you as soon as I can."

6

RESPOND

No man is pleased to have his all neglected, be it ever so little
—DR. SAMUEL JOHNSON, LETTER TO
LORD CHESTERFIELD, 1755

Don't ignore your staff just because you think you can

In your new position you will soon realize that as far as your staff is concerned, you are the first gatekeeper of the company's authority and power. If they have a problem at work, they have to start with you. One way or another you need to take care of it. If your employees start jumping over your head to your own boss, everyone will get upset and you will look bad.

This means that a lot of issues will land on your desk, and it means that unless you act on them, they will lie there. You might feel, quite naturally, that you will get to them in your own time, and to a certain extent this is true: you do not want your speed of response to be dictated by your staff, not least because it is then out of your control. You will have enough control problems from above without getting them from below.

But what you should try to do is respond in a timely fashion. It's not just good business practice or basic courtesy, though these are important. It's showing that you are concerned about what your colleagues say, think and do. This will be appreciated. You don't have to like every idea you hear, you don't have to support every proposal or cause, but you should be seen to be taking it seriously, and not perceived to have forgotten about it. (You would almost certainly not drag your feet when responding to your own boss.)

Every idea from every employee does not deserve to be acted upon immediately, but every idea does deserve acknowledgement. By all means, put it on your own timetable. For example, an idea is sent to you by e-mail. You should respond, saying thanks for the note, you're busy right now, but will get back to them shortly. The sender is assured you have seen the message, and you can now consider it at your own pace. Most importantly, don't be tempted to tacitly remind them who's the boss by ignoring them for days or weeks: They know you are the boss; give them cause to respect your position and not be exasperated by it.

7

THE MASK OF COMMAND

The importance of how you appear to your staff

As the boss, what you say, what you do and how you look are of fundamental importance to your job. Once you become a boss, you have surrendered the ability to pass relatively unnoticed at work. You are always being looked at by your staff—scrutinized is not too strong a word. In corporate America, people at all levels are constantly searching for spoken and unspoken clues about what is happening with the company in general, and particularly their own place within it. The first place they look for clues is to their boss.

For those who work in a large company where senior management is remote, their immediate boss is the most visible embodiment of the company. In addition to being the messenger through which company policy and official information passes, the moods, actions and informal comments of the boss will be harvested by the staff and analyzed for signs of corporate and departmental success or failure.

It would be nice if the boss's mood had no effect on the staff reporting to her. Then she could scream or sulk or pout with impunity, while the rest of the staff blithely took no notice and carried on diligently with their tasks. Unfortunately, that does not happen. When the boss is grumpy and irritable, everyone is nervous and distracted from their work; when the boss laughs, everyone around laughs, and the loudest laughter is often reserved for the boss's jokes. This is a combination of relief born of Byzantine logic: "If he's making jokes in my presence, then that must mean for now he's not planning to fire me," and a sense that the department and company must be doing well –at least for now.

People will look to the boss at all times but especially during difficult situations. That is when your value as a leader will be most clearly on display and therefore, it will be your most testing time.

A British historian, John Keegan, wrote a book about military leadership called *The Mask of Command*. In the book, Mr. Keegan talks of what he calls "the eternal questions" of leadership: "Where is our leader?" "Is he to be seen?" "What does he say to us?" "Does he share our risks?" "Is he in front always, sometimes or never?" In addition to these, here is a question of mine: "How does he appear?"

These questions are just as "eternal" for business leadership. When a crisis happens, don't disappear inside your office: Spend as much time as you can with your colleagues. Be very visible ("Where is our leader . . . Is he to be seen?"). Talk to as many people as possible with positive words of encouragement ("What does he say to us?"). Make sure you look smart and businesslike, and try to keep smiling (How does he appear?"). Your performance as a boss will ultimately be defined and judged by everyone in the company (including your own boss) almost entirely by how you react in crisis situations. You will not be evaluated on how you react and perform when things are going well.

When you become a boss, any public display of your bad humor is a luxury you can no longer afford. Maybe allow yourself a moment of exasperation in the privacy of your office, but once outside you have to put on your public face, and that face must be relentlessly upbeat. That doesn't mean lie about bad situations, but it's your job to point out the silver linings: Your staff can usually imagine enough gloom by themselves.

It's not just to make everyone feel better and less anxious— although that is important, it's also a productivity issue. When there is a crisis, people tend to either stop working completely or work more slowly and less effectively. Keeping morale up will help prevent this paralysis and work will continue to get done.

Here is a short passage taken from Keegan's book. It's a quote from a seventeenth-century Italian general called Raymondo Montecuccoli which succinctly sums up the importance of this chapter. In talking about how a general in the army develops confidence, Montecuccoli says that the general should show that

> He himself is lighthearted and full of hope by means of his facial expressions, his words and his dress. His visage should be severe, his eyes intrepid and luminous, and his clothing flamboyant. He should banter with his men, be clever and witty. They will then deduce that their General could not jest and enjoy himself like that if there were any real danger, if he did not think that he were much stronger or if he did not have good reason to scorn the enemy. The troops are bound to take confidence.

8

KNOW YOUR EMPLOYEES' GOALS

You're not the only one with ambition

You might like to fondly believe that all your staff had reached the pinnacle of their careers and realized their dreams by working for you. Unfortunately—as you secretly know—this is not the case. Although you may prefer not to confront the fact, it's important for everyone that you be aware of your employees' individual aspirations.

It's not easy for an employee to tell her boss she wants to do something different, and so you will rarely find someone who is eager to discuss a job change with you. It's not a very flattering comment, and apart from the concern she could be handicapping her career, it's a reversal of the typical corporate scenario in which it's the boss who is supposed to decide what's best and move people around accordingly.

So if your employees don't willingly offer up their personal ambitions, you will have to take the initiative and find out. You must find the right time, which is usually at the annual review or appraisal. You should ask them carefully, not flippantly such as, "Well, I suppose your next step is to want my job!" You should make it clear that you are interested in what they think so you can help their careers move in the direction they want. You should also make it clear that you don't necessarily have a magic wand to grant them what they wish for. Finally, you should make sure they understand that you like and value having them around, if true, and that you are not looking to chase them off.

It's not a very easy conversation. You will almost certainly be surprised. Some probably *will* want your job. Some will want more money. Some may have a hankering for a different role in your operation. Some may want to move to a completely different area of the company. Some may want to relocate to one of your offices in another part of the country for personal or family reasons (this desire occurs more frequently than you might think).

Hearing a lot of these wishes at around the same time can have a rather daunting effect. It can seem that everyone is anxious to do something else and that they already have one foot out of the door. You might consequently get a bit depressed and think you are doing a terrible job, and that the operation will be left deserted as everyone bails out. But few will have a specific time frame in mind, and in reality most people will not be in a hurry to change.

Even though it's not much fun to hear your key people tell you they want to move on, the alternative—not hearing about it—is much worse. People have their goals whether you ask them or not. If you ignore the issue, many will pursue these goals anyway, and having made their own arrangements they will blindside you with an announcement usually when you least expect it or want it. That is a bad thing: you lose a good person, you must scramble to replace them and your own boss wonders why you let them go.

If, on the other hand, you become part of the process, a lot of good things happen. First and most basic is that by simply asking them, your thoughtfulness will be appreciated, and will probably in itself make some people less willing to leave. If they want to transfer within the whole company, you can begin to facilitate it, but on your own terms. If they want a different role in your own operation, that is something you can more easily arrange—as long as they are qualified and it makes sense. And if they are not ready to switch, then you can work with them to prepare for that change, around which you can build their performance reviews.

There is also a good chance that they may suggest a role for themselves that you hadn't considered but which actually sounds interesting (remember that not every great idea originates with you). The overall effect of these discussions is to put you in control of a potentially uncontrollable situation. It also makes you look like a smart manager, in contrast to the paranoid boss who prays each night that none of his employees ever leave, and then, of course, they all do.

9

BEING LIKED

That's Randolph Churchill's son Winston: I don't like the
fellow but he'll be Prime Minister of England one day.
—SIR GEORGE WHITE, COMMANDER-IN-CHIEF OF INDIA, 1887

Do you want to be liked or do you need to be liked?

To a degree, almost everyone wants to be liked; some people
crave being liked, while others are relatively unconcerned. In
business, being the boss and wanting to be liked is understandable,
but a desperate need to be liked is not compatible with being the
boss.

Although the boss has the power to make people happy, being
the boss inevitably involves upsetting people. Many of the boss's
decisions will result in someone becoming a bit disgruntled, or
worse. This is especially true at salary review time. Some employees
will not get what they want; this makes them unhappy and they
hold the boss responsible.

A boss has to implement corporate policy as well as setting
rules of her own. Much of this involves telling people what they
cannot do, and this will also cause unhappiness.

Successful bosses and leaders either: (1) do not care about
being liked, or, more typically, (2) do care, but don't let it get in

the way of their decision making. These leaders usually don't enjoy upsetting people and prefer it when they don't have to, but neither do they recoil from making unpopular decisions. This liberates them, allowing them to do what they sincerely believe is best for their operation or the company.

You may have been unlucky enough to witness the reverse of this: a boss who is paralyzed by the fear of upsetting people. As a result, unpleasant decisions are fudged or delayed or simply avoided.

If the thought of all this potential unpopularity sounds intimidating, here is something for you to ponder. Most employees don't even *want* a boss who is likable. It certainly helps if the boss is a pleasant enough person, but employees primarily want a boss who is fair and a boss who treats them appropriately and who does all the other things mentioned in greater detail in Chapter 13. Above all, employees want a boss they can respect; they are not looking for a deep, mutually affectionate relationship.

The quote at the top of this chapter is about Winston Churchill. During the years leading up to the Second World War, Churchill consistently took the position that trying to appease Germany in the hope that Hitler would not bother England was a huge error. But many people in England desperately wanted to appease Germany. The First World War was a recent memory, and another terrible conflict was more than they could face. Churchill's position was deeply unpopular: He lost friends and made enemies but he appeared not to care. He was more concerned with doing what he believed was right, undeterred by any effect on his popularity.

10

DON'T COPY YOUR MENTOR

Learn from others, but do it your own way

A good mentor in the corporate world is important. Some people say that without a mentor, corporate advancement is difficult, and it's hard to disagree. It's not easy to get noticed by the top management if you are one of eight thousand employees, so a good mentor can help raise your profile. I have rarely seen a person get a significant promotion without someone commenting, "Oh, he's David's buddy," or people asking, "Who's her big protector?" Talent is important, but unless someone enters you in the talent contest, it's tough to get noticed.

Over time you've probably been observing your mentor and have seen how well she has done. You have learned things from her, hoping to emulate or exceed her success. In your own role as boss, you might encounter a problem and think, "How would my mentor handle this?" "What would she do and say in this situation?" And then it is tempting to do the same thing, or at least the thing you thought she would have done. It's not a bad strategy. The danger is that just as you and your employees are not perfect, neither is your mentor. Simply aping their presumed reaction is therefore not always good. It's one thing to conclude what she would have done, but your next step is to evaluate whether it's the right thing to do in this case. And if it's not, don't do it. Learn from others, certainly, but be your own person, make your own decisions.

I had a longtime boss and mentor who was, in his own way, brilliant. He was very successful, though not everyone liked him. For a long time I applied the "What would he do?" standard to my own conduct, and for some things it worked, and for other things it didn't. One big way it didn't was in the degree of involvement with the employees. His way was to be very hands-off. "If there's a problem, let me know, otherwise I don't need to hear from you." Personally, I quite liked this lack of interference. Perhaps more feedback would have been nice, but he was in New York and I was in Chicago, and on balance it suited me well.

But what worked well for me did not work for the managers who reported to me. They wanted much more involvement, and told me so. What I saw as giving them the room to operate that my boss gave me, they saw as reflecting a lack of interest. Once I realized this, I altered my approach to suit their needs. My mistake was assuming my boss's method was the most desirable; my boss did many things well, but not everything.

11

THE BIG IDEA

Make progress in small ways

For a new manager in a position of relative power, it is an attractive thought that now she will produce a big idea that will revolutionize the way the company does business. This will result in huge profits either by increases in sales, or by cost savings generated by her insightful reappraisal of internal processes.

This is partly due to the fact of being promoted: a sense that the company has recognized her ability, and has not only put her in a position of influence but is expecting great things to happen.

Unfortunately, the reality is more mundane. Rarely are companies catapulted upwards by inspirational strokes of genius. Most successful operations get that way through a lot of hard work, application and some patience. They also get better by continually being reassessed and modified. "If it's not broken don't change it," is not always a good motto. An operation that is willing to constantly examine itself and make adjustments is an operation that normally does well.

For successful companies, genius really is a lot more perspiration than inspiration. As a manager, you need to recognize this early and understand that your own success will usually be accomplished incrementally. Be satisfied with small victories and minor improvements. A process or system slightly streamlined to save some time; a satisfied customer who gives you a nice order but not a record setting order. You are always better off with a large constituency of mid-sized customers than with a handful of temperamental giants.

The "big ideas" tend to come down from the highest level of companies, dreamed up by the executives or sometimes imported from outside consultants. They rarely succeed and are usually viewed by employees as merely the latest fad from the executive office. Even the largest companies are just the sum of their many individual parts, and all these parts will have their own particular challenges that require special attention rather than broad doctrines.

The English author P.G. Wodehouse once said that he wrote only a few hundred words a day, and he conceded that while it might not sound like much, he wrote every day, and pretty soon he had a page, then a chapter, and before long a book. He ultimately wrote over one hundred books. Treat your management role the same; keep looking for small ways to improve, and before too long you will find you have made considerable progress.

12

TAKE YOUR TIME

Avoid rushed decisions just for the sake of speed

When decisions or responses are required from you—as they frequently will be—remember that you are not a quarterback in the National Football League, who has to make a decision and then implement it almost immediately. People applaud good decisions and can usually deal with bad decisions, but they can't stand indecision. This, however, does not mean you have to produce every decision in three seconds.

The image of the quick-fire decision-maker exists more in fiction than reality, where most issues need at least a few minutes of consideration before an answer is given. There may be some perceived strength about barking out an instant solution, but in corporate America there is little that takes place in a vacuum, and unless the problem is simple and has a very narrow scope of ramification, you will always do better to give it some thought. A quick but stupid decision is still a stupid decision when the impact of the speed has dissipated. (I vividly remember the worst boss I ever had trying to force me into an ill-considered reorganization of my operation during a short walk from the office to a restaurant.)

On the other hand, neither should you take forever to mull

over a decision from every angle. Unless you really need to get some extensive opinions from others, a day or two should be enough for most problems. In the workplace, issues usually arise from within familiar subsets: your staff and colleagues; your customers; your prospects and your suppliers. As the boss, you already have an understanding of this landscape and should be thinking of it almost constantly.

It may be a cliché to say you'll sleep on it, but what this really means is that you give yourself time to view the problem with the advantage of a few more hours, and maybe more importantly, away from the often distorting perspective of the office. Just traveling home and being at home can often give you enough balance to make a better decision the next day. There will, of course, be times when a rapid response is needed, and you should not shrink from that challenge, but you are paid and expected to make good decisions, not hasty ones.

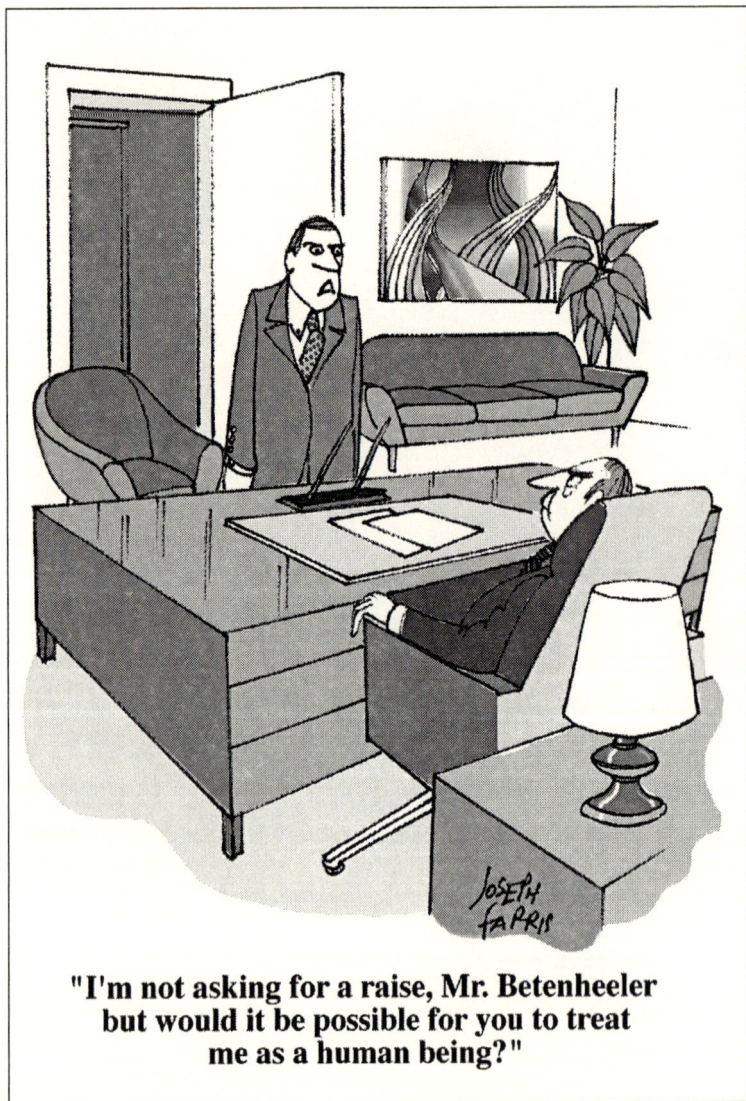

"I'm not asking for a raise, Mr. Betenheeler
but would it be possible for you to treat
me as a human being?"

13

WHAT DO EMPLOYEES CARE ABOUT?

Motivating your staff

In the last chapter, we saw how you don't necessarily have to do much to keep your staff from wanting to leave. But this should not deter you from always trying to make work a better place. This chapter, the longest in the book, discusses many of the things employees care about. To prevent people leaving and to increase your chance of running a successful operation you should pay close attention to these things.

Consistency

Consistency in a boss is a characteristic that is respected by the staff. Even if other criticisms are leveled, people will usually admire consistency. Consistency helps your staff to know where they stand, and where you stand, even though they may not always like it. It is no pleasure always having to guess what the boss will do: your employees should be reasonably sure of what you will do in most situations. Not having this confidence will eventually put a great strain on the employees. Their work will suffer and this will be reflected in the operation's performance.

There are two distinct ways in which you should try to demonstrate consistency. The first is how consistent you are in your treatment of your staff. If it's one rule for Dianne and Phil, but another rule for Andy, you will soon lose respect.

We saw earlier how nothing captures people's attention more than when you are discussing their own careers. The next most watched behavior is how you shape other people's careers. People of equal standing should be seen to receive equal treatment and if you discriminate between peers, it will be soon noticed. Having said that, don't be afraid to make exceptions, if it's appropriate.

One of our assistants was having some problems with her eyes. The dryness in the office air plus staring at the computer screen was causing her eyes to become sore and irritated. She wanted to bring a small humidifier to work and set it in her cubicle. She also had a short note from the optician saying dry air was causing her problems. My first thought, as usual, was how would this sit with the rest of the staff? What precedents will it open up? What will be the next request? What if everyone brought in a humidifier?

My first thought was to say I'm sorry Mary, but it's just not practical. But I thought again. Why shouldn't she have one? Her eyes were hurting and it might help her. Everyone was not going to bring their own humidifier, especially as they would have to buy it themselves and not get it provided by the company.

I was initially being too cautious about being scrupulously consistent. It was appropriate to make a special case exception for Mary. If someone else wanted to bring in something similar, I'd simply look at that request on its own merits, and handle it accordingly. I therefore had a good reason for giving permission, and could explain why I gave it The second way you should demonstrate consistency is in what you do versus what you say. Because everyone scrutinizes your behavior, if what you say is at odds with how you act, you will lose their respect. Nothing you say will be taken completely seriously. This can be something as simple as arriving at work on time. If you are often late, it is a poor idea to criticize your colleagues for doing the same thing.

There is a temptation—not always conscious—to have one law for the employees and one for you. It's a feeling that you should be entitled to some kind of executive privilege, but you get plenty of this privilege by virtue of your title, salary and power: You don't need to have parallel codes of conduct to emphasize it. If you can avoid the charge of hypocrisy, you will do a lot to earn the respect of your staff and keep your operation focused on work rather than on your shortcomings.

On the subject of consistency, there is a larger issue that you should be aware of, even if you can't always do anything about it. This is the problem of corporate hypocrisy, where the stated company policy is one thing, but corporate behavior as demonstrated by the very senior executives is another.

One of the most egregious examples of corporate hypocrisy, and of the impact it can have happened in April 2003 at American Airlines. Like most of the passenger-airline industry, American was suffering badly from a drop off in traffic after the September 11, 2001 terrorist acts, which was then compounded by the Iraqi war of early 2003. The result was that American Airlines lost $5 billion in 2001 and 2002, and a further $1 billion during the first three months of 2003.

Facing bankruptcy, the American Airlines Chief Executive, Donald J. Carty, pressed the unions for huge pay and benefits concessions as the only way to avert bankruptcy. This they agreed to, to help save the company. But while demanding sacrifices from the workers, the American executives were arranging special bonus payments and pension protections for themselves. These executive perks were revealed just as the union voting on the concessions was ending. There was outrage—how could the executives reward themselves while at the same time requiring financial sacrifices from everyone else? It was corporate hypocrisy in the extreme; Donald Carty quickly apologized, but it was not enough. After a week, he was forced to resign as Chairman and Chief Executive Officer.

Corporate hypocrisy is extremely corrosive; if it continues, it will eventually destroy the firm, as the best people will leave. In the case of American Airlines, it cost the chairman his job and nearly pushed the company into bankruptcy.

Fairness

A fair boss is usually a respected boss. While you will inevitably like some of your staff more than others, you should always strive to give everyone an equal opportunity to succeed. It's good for the company, it's good for the employees, and it's good for you.

This is not always easy: corporate life is not always fair, but you should make it apparent that anyone who can perform according to your standards will be welcomed and rewarded. It's hard to conceal from everyone those who you like a lot and those to whom you are neutral; so when one of your "neutral" employees does something good, make sure he or she knows, and make sure everyone else knows how pleased you are.

Treat Your Staff Like Adults

If you have a group of competent workers who can handle most tasks they are given, they will appreciate not being fussed over. There is no need to keep checking on them to see if things are going well. This is harder to do for the new manager who will be anxious to keep a close watch on the whole operation, but if it continues for too long, people will get tired of it.

This is very different from ignoring them. You must make it clear that as soon as they need help or advice, they must ask for it, especially if there is a problem. If they think your distance means you don't care, then you have a bigger problem. Recognize they are adults and can work without constant supervision, but be sure they are comfortable in coming to you for help when it's needed. Maybe by micromanaging everything, you will eventually discover something that could be done a little better, but any such improvement will be minor compared to the benefits you gain by allowing people room to work unsupervised. While most employees do not mind when their boss tells them clearly *what* to do, they have a problem if the boss then tells them *how* to do it.

Equipment

One of the smartest things you can do is give your employees the equipment they need, the support they need, and then stay out of their way! Resist the temptation to stroll into their workspaces in the middle of the morning with a cup of coffee, a friendly smile and a look that says you're going to be there for thirty minutes to "see how things are going."

Chances are that things are going just fine, and will continue to do so if only you go away. Even your best people need your leadership, guidance, praise and attention, but often the best way you can help your star performers is to ensure that they have the tools they need to do their job.

These days, this often means technology, hardware and software. If they send a lot of faxes, get a good system that enables them to fax from their computers. If they print a lot of documents, see that there are enough good printers so they don't have a two-minute trip whenever they want to print and collect something. See that their computers are fast enough. It's easy to keep your capital budget low and make your expenses look good by not buying new equipment, but your staff will not appreciate it and productivity will suffer.

Support also means furniture: ergonomic chairs, enough filing cabinets, coffee machines, and the whole physical infrastructure of an office. Some of the loudest complaining from our best people (who rarely complained) came when the coffee machine broke down, or when the sugar supply kept running out due to misplaced parsimony. It was as if there had been a breach in an unspoken contract. They would work hard, but we had to make sure the coffee didn't run out.

It also means good lighting; if the building lights are inadequate, get them desk lamps. And be sensitive to noise levels and traffic patterns that create distractions.

Letting everyone know you are committed to getting the right equipment is almost as crucial as actually getting it. Also, make sure you can at least talk intelligently about the equipment. Do not display a blasé attitude about the equipment that is fundamental to the work of your employees: show them you are concerned about it, that you know how important it is, and you are always looking to improve it.

Support also means appropriate people. This is difficult as people are always the most expensive support item. Now that everyone is a keyboard operator, the type of support needed has changed, but there will still be support tasks to be done, and you do not want your best people doing them.

Control

A behavioral study was once conducted in which a group of people were put in a room, and asked to solve a problem. The twist was that they were subjected to intrusive and distracting noises while they were doing it. Not surprisingly, the noise irritated them and their ability to perform the task was reduced.

Another group was put in the same situation, but this group was told that if they wanted to, they could shut off the noise. They proceeded to outperform the other group. The interesting thing is that they did not actually shut the noise off: merely knowing that they could stop it if they wanted was sufficient for them to disregard it. They were in control of the nuisance, so they could live with it.

This illustrates an important characteristic of corporate employees: They like to feel they have control. They don't necessarily have to exercise that control, or actually have control, just feel that they do. A worker whose working life is beyond his or her control is usually a stressed and unhappy person. It's hard for them to plan their day as they are always at the mercy of others. At the lower end of the corporate hierarchy, you will find these people searching for ways to take back some control. How do they achieve it? Look at the cubicles of your most junior colleagues, and see how they have personalized them with pictures, banners, souvenirs, objects. They are demonstrating their control in one of the few areas that they can: their work-space.

How else do they do it? Less innocently than workspace decorations, they are the ones who know exactly how many sick days they are allowed and always take them. Find ways to give your staff some control over their destiny, hopefully real control, but if not, then perceived. Involve them in some decisions, as far as possible leave them to control how they spend their day. Don't fence in your employees to such an extent that it's miserable for them.

Include not Exclude

People in general, and at work in particular, like to feel included. At work, it can cause paranoia: "I'm not invited to lunch! Everyone else is going and I'm not! Am I being fired? Does this mean I will not get a raise?" In corporate America, when people don't include you, it says, "You don't matter," even if the circumstances are inconsequential, and people need to feel that they do matter.

Of course, you can't include everyone in everything, but you should realize that every time you call a meeting, grab some colleagues for lunch or do anything that involves a group, someone is probably going to feel excluded. Some of this you can shrug off, and certainly, if you agonize too much you'll be paralyzed and achieve nothing; just be aware of it.

When you call a meeting, try to invite anyone who has a direct and meaningful interest in the subject matter (without tying up too many people). This leads to fewer misunderstandings, and fewer people left unhappy at being on the wrong side of the conference room window.

Make them Feel Special

Everyone wants to feel that they are special. If you work for a huge company, it's hard for people to feel that they are special, at almost any level. The more you can neutralize this feeling of being expendable, the more your employees will appreciate it. Even with the best intentions, it is difficult for the CEO of a large company to make everyone feel special. That means that it's up to you as a middle manager to compensate for the CEO not being accessible. To your employees, you embody the company and are the surrogate CEO, and so however distant the real CEO might appear, you can do a lot to reduce any sense of alienation.

Information Sharing

Even though information in the corporate world has become

more democratized, there is still a lot of internal knowledge possessed by the boss that she can decide whether or not to share with the staff. A good boss will share as much information as possible, while a bad boss will protect it. The more information you can share, the better your staff will feel. There should be little that you absolutely cannot pass on that is related to the business.

Clearly, individual personnel issues and data are strictly confidential, as is any knowledge that your own bosses have forbidden you to divulge. Beyond that, share the information: people perform better in such an environment.

Morale

Bad morale in the workplace is like an overweight person: It did not take three weeks for him to put on fifty pounds, and it's not going to take only three weeks for him to lose it. Just as emergency diets seldom work for long, emergency measures to improve morale never last very long either. You may have heard of corporate weekend retreats to improve morale, with games and tests and sometimes ordeals. All these are like the emergency diet and are about as effective. They are usually organized by managers who realize morale is bad, do not realize that they may be largely responsible, and go for a drastic cure. Morale did not get bad in one weekend, and will not be fixed in the same time period.

Morale goes bad through insensitivity to the subjects discussed in this chapter and through prolonged and repeated cynical acts by the management. Add to this the poor communication between boss and employees, and you have a situation where all the good people want to leave. It is your challenge as boss to see that, as far as possible, these conditions are eliminated or at least minimized, and try to keep morale as high as you can.

Postscript

In general, employees do not care for a boss who shouts, uses bad language or is particularly short tempered. A boss who displays these characteristics will often have an unhappy workforce who will put up with it only as long as they have to.

Another point to remember is that if you are normally a well-mannered boss but for some reason act in a rude or offensive way, you will almost certainly feel very bad about it afterwards. Apart from any discomfort felt by the person who is the object of your anger, you will feel that you have let yourself down by your behavior, and the unpleasant memory of it will never really disappear. If this happens, then the best thing to do is apologize as soon as you can. It will probably be well received and is not a sign of weakness.

Unless it's part of a strategy designed to galvanize everyone's attention, losing your temper makes you appear out of control. Anger usually makes you say stupid things and act stupidly.

14

ELEPHANTS AND EMPLOYEES

Be careful what you tell your staff about their careers

It is a feature of the workplace that people will easily forget all sorts of things, often relatively important things, but they will never forget anything that you, the boss, tell them about their careers. Therefore, it is vital that such discussions consist of comments that you absolutely believe to be true, and promises that you are prepared to fulfill when your colleague repeats them almost word for word in eight months time.

Actually, it's even harder than that, because not only will they recall the conversations, they will sometimes edit them to suit their own purposes. So in addition to saying only what you want them to hear, you have to make it as unambiguous as possible. This is not always easy. Here is a true example.

A woman came to see me about a business issue, and after we had discussed that, she asked if she could change the subject to that of working from home. She then asked if at some time in the future the company would allow people to work from home for all or part of the week. There were no plans that I knew to allow this, but adopting standard corporate language, I said that given the way business was changing, and given the advances in technology, I would not be surprised if perhaps at some time in the future, maybe in a year or two, the company tried some kind of pilot scheme to see how it worked. Non-committal enough, I thought. I was therefore surprised to receive an e-mail from the woman a day or so later volunteering to be part of the pilot scheme. She had overlooked the qualifying words "perhaps," "maybe," "a year or two," and had drawn the conclusion that we were already looking for volunteers. I do not think she was being disingenuous: I think she really believed that was how the conversation went.

What I should have said was that the company had no plans for anyone to work from home and that it was not an option. I made the mistake of trying to soften the truth, and paint a more congenial picture for her benefit (and mine). Instead, I should have kept it uncompromisingly factual. When it comes to career comments, be careful. If you make a casual remark to a good employee that if she continues to perform at this level she'll be a vice-president within a couple of years, she will mark her calendar for exactly two years time, when she will expect that title.

It is tempting to make pleasantries in passing about someone's career, but you should try to resist it, especially during a formal appraisal or performance review. Say only what you really mean and say it with unambiguous clarity. Imagine you are conducting the appraisal of a good performer, currently an assistant vice-president who wants to know when he can expect to move up to vice-president. If you commit to a time frame, you must be confident that you can deliver on your promise. This could involve getting the blessing of your own boss who may have to approve such promotions, so you must also be prepared to argue on behalf of your staff if you believe they deserve it.

15

FOLLOW THE LEADER

Like it or not, the boss is always a role model

All animals need to be survivalists and humans are no different. In the deceptively civilized environment of corporate America, the instinct to survive and prosper is as strong as anywhere. It might not involve physical force, but strategic maneuvering to gain an advantage is constant.

Because the boss holds such sway over the careers of the people reporting to her, pleasing the boss is an important goal of most employees and the primary goal for many. This can often be at the expense of doing good work. One of the more accurate criticisms leveled against a former company was that the people in the New York home office judged good work not by how effective it was in helping the enterprise, but whether or not the senior management *thought* it was good work.

An easy way to please a boss is to act like her. If the boss gets to work early, then people will try to show up around the same time. If the boss is often late, then punctuality is deemed less important. The staff will take fashion cues from the boss, man or woman. When you are the boss, your employees study every action you take so they can learn the acceptable behavioral benchmarks and then copy them.

This might all seem straightforward, but its importance should be emphasized, because it applies to everything you do. All your actions, mannerisms, habits will set the tone for everyone who reports to you. If you want your staff to be ethically beyond reproach, then you had better be that way yourself. If you act like a slob, then don't be surprised to see it imitated. You like to take long lunches? So will your staff.

If you want your staff to be interested in something, then you had better make sure that you are interested in it, and are seen to be interested in it. Note also that in addition to the survivalist instinct of wanting to please you for the sake of advancement, the younger staff members will look up to you as a role model, whether you want them to or not. Some, in a modest way, will even idolize you: You are in position they aspire to.

Even when you think no one is paying attention to what you are doing, someone almost certainly is: it's a big responsibility that many bosses underestimate.

16

A SOUNDING BOARD

Test out your ideas before you take them public

As much as you try to keep your ear to the ground, inevitably there will be many things that you will not hear about. This is partly a function of your position as boss; few people make a point to let you know what's happening at the grass roots, and partly because if you are doing your job well you won't have time because you will be very busy. You may find that people who might have gossiped before you were boss will now choose not to, because of the changed relationship.

This could potentially lead to an intelligence gap, which you don't want. Even if a lot of the stuff you are missing is trivial, mixed in are valuable pieces of opinion and moods that you need to know. Like a lot of intelligence, you might discount it or ignore it, but first you have to discover it.

What you need is someone to confide in. Historically, the boss's secretary or assistant has taken this role and this is still the best person for the job. If you do have a personal assistant, and you are only using her for booking flights, restaurants, typing and other clerical functions, you are under-utilizing her. Not only can she pass back to you valuable insights into the mood of the office, she can also act as an informal conduit of your feelings back to the office.

In addition to passing back these informal comments to the staff, your assistant can also be used as a sounding board to test out ideas before you plunge ahead. This does not only mean your assistant's own opinion, although that is valuable, but the general mood of the office. Just as your assistant is your confidant, she in turn will have a couple of confidants, all of whom will give you indirect feedback.

If you don't have your own assistant, you will have to cultivate someone else. However, don't expect them to volunteer information. Because of a natural aversion to sucking up to the boss, you will have to extract it: "Jim, what do people really think of the new filing system? What are the problems? Am I missing something?" If prodded enough, most people will talk.

One important note of caution: Don't become so conspiratorial with your assistant that your senior managers and colleagues feel they are being excluded. Most good assistants are extremely loyal and supportive, and it can be tempting—even therapeutic—to over-confide in them. Even the best assistants should not be substitutes for your professional colleagues. Be careful of even giving the appearance that you are treating your senior staff as outsiders, denied privileged information and having their status relegated.

17

FIRING

An unpleasant but unavoidable subject

Sooner or later, preferably sooner, you will have to fire someone. It's preferable to do it sooner rather than later because it is an inevitable part of corporate life, these days more than ever. And the earlier in a manager's career it happens, the better, so that years don't pass and the prospect becomes more dreaded.

There is a type of dismissal that usually accompanies a merger or acquisition known as a Reduction in Force, or RIF. While there are often some merit factors involved in such cases, they can also involve people who really do not deserve to go, and as such are usually beyond the control of the middle manager. We will, therefore, not address this situation.

The dismissal at issue here is one of performance. The actual mechanics of the process will not be discussed. Most companies have a very specific procedure and you must have to stick to it. What I'm going to discuss is some of the internalizing that you will go through.

First of all, make sure that you are completely convinced it is the right decision for the operation. It is a huge step from wishing someone were gone to actually getting rid of them. Be sure it really is because of performance, and that personality issues are not the driving force; be sure you have considered every other option and have kept the Human Resources department apprised.

Having made the decision, act quickly. Most managers wait too long, not wanting to face the reality of the situation. They will make excuses for someone's poor performance; they will hope for improvement, they may even, as I once did, implement a whole system precisely in an attempt to instill discipline and good habits into someone who lacked them. In that instance it was a lot of wasted effort and just dragged things out an extra year.

As you mull it over, bear in mind these three things. First, if you are worried about being fair, then reverse the situation and ask yourself if not firing the person is fair to the rest of the staff. They are all doing a good job and probably carrying the person either directly or indirectly. Is it fair to them to bear this burden and have them subsidize the under-performer? Second, remember that your employees usually know better than you who is a good worker and who isn't. You will usually come to that conclusion some time after they have all figured it out. They know who is not pulling their weight and deserves to go, and the longer the person is kept on, the more their respect for you will diminish. Third, if it's the right thing, then you will probably still feel somewhat awful before you do it, but you will definitely feel relieved and better when it's done.

18

DATA

Control it, and ask for it selectively

As a new boss, you will now be directly involved in the flow of corporate data. It used to that one of a manager's main functions was to receive information and disseminate it downwards, usually on an imperious "need to know basis." This still happens, but the vast amount of data now accessible by individuals from the Internet have democratized knowledge and rendered this part of the manager's job if not obsolete, then certainly less important. It is one of the reasons that middle managers have been struggling with their changing identity as their role as dispenser of information is being diminished. Knowledge is still power, but having less control of the knowledge has implicitly eroded middle managers' position. In the "old days," the manager typically got all the trade periodicals first and then passed them on. Now, it is the most junior staff member who is likely to dig up something interesting on the Internet and circulate to the department via e-mail.

While your role in passing down information might be reduced, you will still need to request internal data such as reports and numbers. Good data has always been important to management: "If you can't measure you can't manage," is correct.

To talk meaningfully to customers, you need accurate data of your past and present transactions with them. The same thing applies with suppliers. In dealing with both sides of the business equation, people who buy from you and people who sell to you, you need data—and the better your data, the stronger will be your leverage in these discussions.

Internally, you need data on your staff, anything they do that is measurable. There is sometimes resistance to using hard data in evaluating employees. You'll hear about extenuating circumstances, the special reasons why Fred's numbers are not as good as Susie's. There is sometimes validity in this, but make sure you get the data first and then listen to the arguments. The best people usually produce the best numbers; they find ways to get things done and succeed. The less effective people usually produce less impressive numbers.

Get control of the data, for inside and outside purposes, especially financial data. Make sure you know where the money comes from and how it's being spent. This sounds obvious, but many managers have only a vague idea of these details. Look at expense reports and make sure people know you are reading them. Sooner or later, your company will go on a cost-cutting mission and your own boss will be pestering you for accurate expense information. The more familiar you are with these numbers, the quicker you can respond.

If you are an internal service provider with internal customers, data will be equally critical. It might even be more so because of the tendency of internal customers to hold their in-house providers to a higher standard. Having good, relevant and topical data in these situations is vital.

It's also important to be familiar enough with the data that you know how to put your own particular interpretation on it. This applies both upwards when presenting data to your own boss and downwards when you discuss how it impacts individuals who report to you. This doesn't just mean current data but historic data as well. Here is a simple example. Your own boss comments that one of your employees has had an unproductive year compared to his peers. Instead of saying nothing or weakly agreeing, you should acknowledge that fact, but then be able point to the individual's outstanding record for the past three years. Having established that this is a proven performer, you can then explain the specific reasons why this year is not so productive.

When you ask for reports and data, you are usually asking your systems and finance colleagues to do the work. Try to avoid asking for data that you will probably never use. A former colleague had a phrase for it. He called unused requests for data, "curiosity requests" because his boss would say something like, "Out of curiosity, how many sales calls did we make in Detroit between April and July last year?" My colleague would then spend all morning scrambling to get the data, pass it on, and never hear anything further.

By making such aimless requests, you will alienate the people who have to gather the data, and so when you really do want something quickly, it might not get the attention you need. It is tempting to use your new power as boss to ask for "curiosity" data: resist it. Before you request reports, you should have a clear idea of why you want them and how you will use them. It is a good idea to tell the data-gatherers exactly why you want the information. First, they may know how to get the same thing more efficiently, and second they will appreciate being made part of the whole process.

I was once on the receiving end of a "curiosity" request so bizarre that had it not happened to me, I might have doubted its truth. The job of my operation was to place commercial insurance for large businesses, and we placed this insurance using an array of different insurance companies. One day, a very, very senior executive sent around a message (the only thing I ever saw from him) requesting that we rank the leading insurance companies in terms of competitive pricing, scope of coverage offered, customer service and claims responsiveness. This request went out nationwide to anyone running an operation that worked with insurance companies—not too unreasonable, you might think. But instead of a numerical ranking or even an alphabetical ranking that could be translated to a quantitative score, we had to grade the companies by color. I think red was the best; maybe blue the worst with various colors in between. (I should mention that my company had been acquired by its biggest rival, and I was now trying to fathom a completely foreign senior management team.)

Rank by color? Every insurance company had regional offices, so each one would be graded separately, but what could you possibly do with the findings? A company might be ranked red in Atlanta, blue in New York, yellow in Chicago and green in Los Angeles. How do you then obtain an overall picture? Mix the colors? I called in some team leaders and explained what was needed. Their incredulous responses and our subsequent mockery of the plan were fun, but I still had to complete the profiles. Feeling that this was a complete waste of time, I plugged in some colors, and sent it back. Not surprisingly I never heard anything more; it was a good example of meaningless data that took time to gather and was never used.

Curiosity requests not only take an emotional toll, they involve a financial cost as well: tying up people for useless work ultimately costs money and is bad business. Thinking carefully before you ask for data will also help control the piles of paper gathering dust on your desk.

19

OLDER THAN YOU

Managing an Older Employee

In high school and college, seniority is fairly well determined. The older you are, the more senior you are. This is especially so at American colleges where the four years are not simply referred to neutrally as first, second third or fourth (as in the U.K. for example), but are given specific names: freshman, sophomore, junior, senior. A senior heavily outranks a freshman, even though they are only four years apart in age.

In the workplace, however, precise distinctions are blurred. Seniority is not a rigid function of age, but becomes a function of subjective factors such as perceived ability, favoritism and politics. Initially, it may seem to the entry-level graduate that little is different, and she will usually accept starting as the low person in the organization. But fairly soon she will become aware that just because people have been working there for ten years does not necessarily make them better or more valuable employees.

In the work environment therefore, it is quite normal for the new boss to be managing people older than her. Even though the new boss will probably have seen this happen elsewhere in the company, it can still be intimidating. How the new boss handles these relationships is important, and extra care should be taken.

First, she should recognize that while Bill has clearly reached a plateau in his career and no longer expects to be running the company, this was probably not always so. As a young recruit, Bill may have been just as ambitious as his new boss. While he has probably learned to accept the failure of his dreams to materialize, the gradual erosion of his status as he was repeatedly passed over for promotion has taken its toll.

In these situations, there are some things that the new boss should definitely not do, such as make facetious jokes about Bill's age, which only highlights his failure as well as being impolite—and also may set the company up for an age-discrimination lawsuit.

What the boss must do above all is allow Bill to retain his dignity. Treat him as an older statesman who still has a lot to contribute (he often does), make a special effort to seek his opinion and advice, even if it's not always taken. Bill will understand that the boss does what the boss wants—he's seen it happen often enough, but to at least be consulted during the process means a lot. In Bill's case, all that the company can do for him now (apart from keeping him employed) is pay him more money; promotion will not happen, so retaining dignity and respect means a great deal.

Not only will treating Bill with extra courtesy benefit their relationship, it will attract approval from the rest of the staff. They will, unless Bill is especially disliked, sympathize with Bill's position, and will be watching carefully to see how the new boss handles things. A flippant lack of respect will be frowned upon by the others.

A new boss will sometimes make that mistake out of sheer nervousness; it's a weird thing to be in charge of someone who may be old enough to be your father, and it goes against those social norms of your early years. Being too lighthearted is sometimes a defense against the perceived unnaturalness of the situation, but don't do it. No one will think you are clever, just someone who has been promoted too quickly.

Perhaps most pragmatically of all, in addition to being able to help you a little, Bill can almost certainly hurt you. His original peers who moved ahead in the company probably still talk to him, and a critical word from Bill might set your career back or even derail it. On the other hand, praise from Bill may help boost your career, as you are seen as someone who can handle the challenge of supervising an older person.

A final note of caution: The day you were promoted might be the day that a future batch of "Bills" was created—peers of yours who perhaps hoped for that job but were passed over. Some will move on in other directions, but for a few, your advancement may have sealed their fate. You should be as aware of their situation as you are of Bill's.

20

YOU CAN'T LOVE EVERYTHING

Your staff are not perfect and neither are you

As a new boss, you want everything to be perfect and everyone to act perfectly. If promoted from within the operation (which is where most first-time bosses come from), you will start to see colleagues in a different light. A former peer who is now a subordinate suddenly has problems where before he had amusing foibles.

Those long lunches that you took before you were promoted now cause you irritation when it's someone else returning at around three o'clock. What used to seem an enjoyable and harmless excursion, you now see as impacting productivity. It will be especially annoying when you need to see him urgently and he's still at lunch.

This is a problem you had never noticed before because, of course, you were not the manager then. One of our best managers had a habit of storing up lots of tiny issues, such as wanting to re-design the fax forms or moving a filing cabinet, and then sending me the whole list by e-mail, demanding that we do something about all this as soon as possible, and how we had to "get organized." This behavior seems unexceptional, until it's you who is on the receiving end, and have to deal with it.

In your first months as the new boss, it is likely you will find that everyone has some kind of behavioral habit that you'd like to change. Being the boss, and being new to the experience, you might think that you could use your authority and do something about it. Refraining from taking instant action is a smart move.

The reality is that you can't like everything your colleagues do or say, and in most cases you will just have to find a way to accept it. Look at your friends. Do you like everything they do and say? It's unlikely, but do you end the friendship because of it? Just as your friends are not perfect, neither are your staff.

For a new boss, there is a strong urge to micromanage the operation and the people. The successful boss will determine those things that are irrelevancies and accept them and those things that really do have to be addressed, and take action.

The sooner you can control your annoyance at small, unimportant things, the more relaxed you will be in your position and you will do a better job. Experienced managers have learned to this: They focus quickly on what matters and ignore what really doesn't. And while you are lamenting the lack of perfection in your staff, remember that from their perspective you will hardly be the perfect boss. One cause of an effective workplace is a mutually pragmatic acceptance of everyone's minor failings.

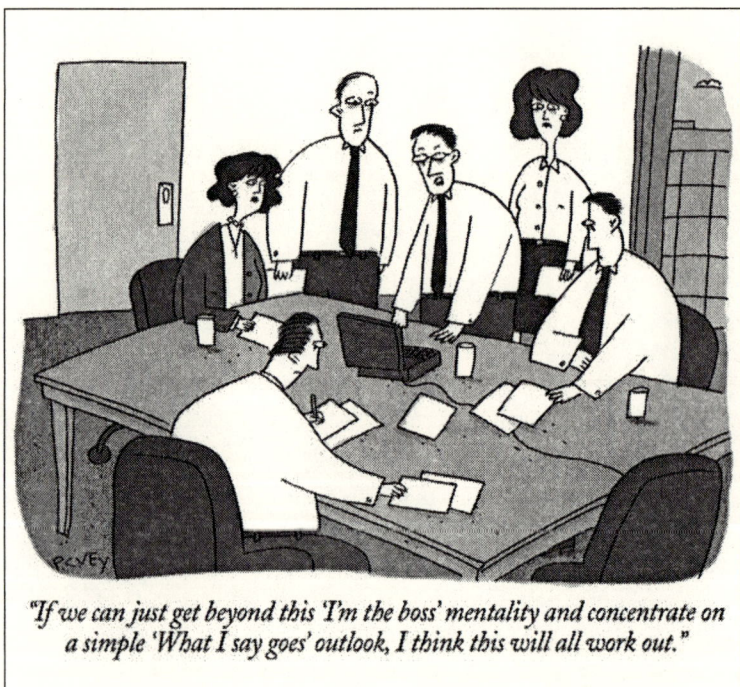

"If we can just get beyond this 'I'm the boss' mentality and concentrate on a simple 'What I say goes' outlook, I think this will all work out."

21

IT'S NOT A DEMOCRACY

Leaders need to make decisions

In business, decisions must be made, and the boss has to make them. If you let everything be discussed by teams or committees and then allow decisions to be made by committee, your staff and more importantly your own boss will start to wonder what you are really there for. Exercising your authority is vital. First, because decisions get things moving, second, because it reminds people of why you are there, and third, because people actually like it. Employees really want the boss to act like the boss—not unpleasantly, by being rude, boorish and offensive—but they do want action. They don't want uncertainty or procrastination. They can live with most decisions, even if they don't always agree with them, but they do not want indecision.

A lot of employee worries in corporate life are vague, and rooted in hypothetical circumstances. Imaginary problems always loom larger and more menacingly than real problems. For example, "If Mark gets to work on that project and not me, then he'll probably be better positioned for promotion than I will." Or, "Now that they hired Alice maybe she'll end up taking my job!" If the boss allows such paranoia to flourish by not being firm and clear, people will get hopelessly distracted. Speculation is very easy, and is usually a waste of everyone's time. By acting decisively and without unnecessary delay, the boss can squash many hypothetical complaints and corrosive worrying with a description of the real world. When there is change, tell the staff individually or collectively that this is the way things are going to be. You might be surprised at how the firmer you are the less anxiety and quibbling there usually is.

Striking the balance between paying too much attention to staff input and being a dictator is something you must manage yourself. You should always welcome input, but you are not presiding over a democracy: Take note of any consensus but then make your own decision. Avoid taking a vote; voting is a clumsy way to register opinion. All a vote can do is to reflect a "yes" or a "no." Most business issues are various shades of gray, but voting usually reduces them to black or white

Anna Wintour, the very successful editor-in-chief of American *Vogue* magazine, succinctly summarizes the crucial role of the boss as the decision maker. In an interview with *The New York Times* (February 17, 2003), Ms. Wintour comments, "I try to be open to other points of view, but people look to you for a decision, and it's most helpful to make one. Even when you aren't completely sure." Exactly.

22

SURVIVAL OF THE FITTEST

Employee triage

Most companies are interested in having only the most competent people work for them. Companies, as a rule, are not interested in providing a cozy place for the nice, but less competent workers to exist, because companies generally have to make a profit, and to make a profit they have to be reasonably successful, and to be reasonably successful they need mostly good people.

This all may seem clear enough, but it's worth emphasizing because you will be faced with financial performance challenges that you can meet only if you have enough good people. As it is unlikely that all your people are good enough, you will have to face the prospect of winnowing them out. A popular approach is to start by dividing the staff into "A," "B," and "C" categories.

Here is a typical description of the three categories:

The "A's" are the ones you want to keep at almost any cost. They help define your organization by their work ethic, their performance and their attitude. These are the people you would go to great lengths to keep happy and you bend the rules to retain because you know your success depends upon them sticking around. They are the people whom you take care of at raise and bonus time, they are the people you go to when you need things done—which they always manage to do, even though they are always the busiest people.

The next one is the "B" group. They are usually the largest of the three groups. They are not "A" people, but maybe could be. They are the ones with promise, fairly good work habits, who help the operation to move along rather than hinder it. They need more of your help and tend to look for it. They will tie up more of your time than the "A" people, but you don't really mind because they are basically worth keeping. Under bad leadership they could stagnate, and perform at a level jus thigh enough to prevent them from being fired. Inspiring these people is one of your biggest challenges.

The "C" category consists of people whom you have little interest in keeping. They are a drag on the enterprise. They are the ones who cause most of your personnel problems, who can, if you let them, tie up much of your time. Their work is poor and their attitude is worse. Occasionally, you will find a good performer with a bad attitude. It's tempting to excuse the bad attitude because of the performance, but that's evading the reality, which is that the negative impact they produce is never worth it.

Just as you are trying hard to keep the "A" group happy, you should be trying to move the "C" group out. It is not a time for sentiment; you are acting on behalf of the whole operation. Only the fittest and most productive can help you achieve your targets, and so only they should survive, for everyone's sake. You should be careful when assigning people to the "C" list. Doing so means that you have spent time and effort trying to get improvement but have not succeeded. In addition, "C" performers do not always drift down from being lower "B's." They can sometimes look like "A' performers.

Here is an example. When I joined a company as a new recruit, there was a person who took me under his wing, introduced me around and taught me many aspects of the business; he was regarded as a key employee. A year later, when I became his boss, I saw for the first time what a shambles his work was in. If he did not want to do something, he simply put it off. Unfortunately, there were many things he did not want to do. Our customers were furious. I tried to change his habits and behavior, but to no avail. In the end, we dismissed him; he was a "C" masquerading as an "A."

However, while the categorizing and the winnowing may be a recognized, standard approach, in reality things are different. Even though removing all the under-performers makes perfect sense, you will find that not only is it hard to do, it can sometimes be actually unhelpful.

The first problem with culling the "C's" (admittedly not the worst problem you could have) is that you are left with a team of high caliber "A" players and some "B" players. You will probably be unable to keep them all happy, either with enough challenging work or with enough money. If your overall budget for salary increases is five percent, and all your "A" players deserve about twice that, what do you do? The "B's" certainly deserve no less than the five percent average. The answer is you take it from the "C's," so one immediate tangible benefit of having a few underperformers is that they can be treated as pure "headcount." You give them no raise, take their five percent, and give it to the achievers.

Second, if you are constantly firing people in your unceasing attempt to eliminate all weak performers, morale suffers. It suffers even among the "A's." Bear in mind that some "A's" will have a degree of self-doubt, and unless you constantly tell them how good they are, they will worry about their own status in an environment of constant upheaval. And if word gets out—as it will—that your goal is to eliminate the bottom ten percent each year, who knows if it will be their turn next. Sure, they might have had a good year, but what about next year? Suddenly, no one feels secure. What can happen then is that the best people take off for a more forgiving environment, leaving you with a bunch of par and sub-par employees that you have to keep because you are now short-staffed.

Appealing though it sounds to have nothing but stars on the payroll, the stars actually need to have some lesser lights dotted around to make them feel secure, and as a means of occasional comparison whereby the stars can reconfirm their ascendancy. In any corporate workplace, there are always some dull tasks to be done; if everyone expects the glamorous assignments, who will do the grunt work?

Even though a certain elite group might do most of the productive work, it's not *all* done by them. By cutting too deep you can find you've sliced off more than you intended. The under-achievers can actually perform a useful function by doing the less critical work or the dull work, as well as accepting small or no raises.

Clearly, if someone is consistently and woefully unproductive, then that's different: they should go. For the rest of those less than stellar performers, I suggest keeping in mind three "M's": Minimize the amount of your time and the operation's money these people take up, Marginalize them so they don't interfere with and handicap your best performers, and Monitor them in case they get so bad they really do have to go. This will often create a situation so uncomfortable for these people that they leave anyway, but that is much better than an annual ten percent cull.

However good your star performers might be, you should never build the operation around them and therefore make them almost irreplaceable. The real star of any organization should be the organization itself. Star performers are good to have, but they should be stars within the system; star performers come and go, but your operation must be able to withstand their departure and keep moving on. Star performers should shine because the operation you have created allows them to shine; stars should not shine in spite of the operation.

23

WRITE IT DOWN

Keep good records, and insist everyone else does

One of the first things you should do is establish a culture of good record-keeping. Anything of the remotest significance should be committed to paper and kept in the appropriate file. Failure to record decisions, discussions and transactions often leads to bad things. Even when no misunderstanding is intended, the impression that two or more people get from a verbal exchange is usually different, and the difference increases with time. More sinister is the fact that some people will actively try to misinterpret unrecorded exchanges to suit their purpose: "Oh, I thought that you were going to do that! I didn't realize it was me!" Internally, such confusion is mostly just inconvenient but externally such misunderstandings can be more serious: "Oh, no, that's not the final price—I thought I had made that clear last week when we spoke."

Even though putting everything in writing can sometimes be tiresome, it helps eliminate intended and unintended ambiguity. The ideal policy is zero tolerance: If it's not written down, then it never happened. This is hard, but it is worth at least aiming for. Anyone who has had the exasperating experience of searching through old files that are incomplete and incomprehensible understands this. The absence of a clear, written record leaves you feeling helpless as you try to discern people's intent from a few scratchy notes, oblique comments and the inevitable doodles. Gaps in the written record that seemed inconsequential at the time can look like black holes years later.

Although the best documenters are usually among your best performers, not all your best performers are good documenters; this is something you will need to work with them on. You will usually find that your bad performers hate the written record. Bad performers thrive in a twilight world of verbal suggestions, fuzziness and ambivalence that keeps them from being pinned down and identified as weak. In a culture where the written record is not viewed as important, these people flourish. A good, written record policy, on the other hand, shines a light into their world and makes them very uncomfortable. Almost as important as the actual act of committing things to writing is the tone of the documentation: People should compose their notes as if they will one day be read out in a court of law. A very good example of how this can come back to haunt you emerged early in 2003 from the firm of Merrill Lynch, the nation's largest stockbroker. Internal e-mail messages containing vulgarisms were produced in the harsh glare of a criminal prosecution. The content—analysts deriding stocks that they were simultaneously pushing clients to buy—was damning, but the unpleasant tone served to reinforce the squalid image.

Record keeping is also helpful with internal corporate issues. Creating a written policy on casual dress is a chore, but if you do not do it you will find that people's own interpretation will fill the vacuum and you will have more trouble correcting it later than setting the standard earlier. Make a record quickly; between the time everyone has left the meeting and the time when the written record gets circulated, the perceived proceedings will be passed on informally. The longer you wait to furnish the official version, the more inaccurate the interpretations become.

24

An Asset Can Become a Liability

Don't get seduced by your own strengths

It's reasonable to assume that among the reasons you got to be the boss was because you have certain talents. You know what these talents are, and you know your shortcomings. You do your best to display these talents; however, there is a possibility that having a particularly prominent skill can actually become a negative force.

Here are some examples. Let's say you are a good listener. This is a rare quality and one that is much appreciated; most people would rather talk than listen. The problem is that as the boss you can take it to extremes, and be only too willing to hear everyone's point of view. But a boss has to talk as much as listen, and if all you appear to do is listen, your good listening will eventually be seen as a weakness.

Here is an example of the reverse problem. One of my bosses was very articulate. He had a gift for crystal-clear explanations and seemed to know something about everything. His voice was strong and when he talked people initially marveled at his verbal skills and broad knowledge. The trouble was, he could never stop talking. Instead of harnessing and using this ability as a valuable tool, his overuse of this talent turned him into an over-informed bore. Had he been able to mix his speaking skills with appropriate listening, he would have commanded great respect and been more successful. It's especially tempting for a boss who is a good talker to talk a lot because the employees are an automatic and usually eager audience: Everyone listens when the boss speaks.

A boss who has an aptitude for numbers may see everything in numerical terms, often appropriate, but not always. Someone who has great writing skills may try to put everything in writing. This is usually good practice in business, but not every management issue is best addressed by a circularized e-mail or lengthy memo; a quick meeting and a message delivered verbally can often be more effective.

Turning one's strength into a handicap is damaging for anyone in business but particularly the boss. Recognizing and addressing this potential problem is a hard thing to do, because it involves a conscious shift from your natural and preferred behavior (as Mark Twain once said, when you are a hammer, everything looks like a nail) but you have to try.

25

Keep Work Appropriate

Respect everyone's role in the operation

One of the most sinking feelings I used to have was to arrive at work and watch the elevator doors open on a dark lobby. This meant that the receptionist had not shown up. It also meant that I would spend the next hour scrambling to draft someone from the ranks of the technical assistant support staff to fill in on the switchboard.

The role of the receptionist / switchboard operator is an important one for most companies; good bosses realize this, but the technical support staff did not. Having a staff member fill in for switchboard duty was for them a triple nuisance. First, they did not like doing it because it was dull. Second, they fell behind with their own work and third, to be on the "board" was a badge of inferiority in their eyes and their peers. They felt it sent a message to everyone in the company that they were expendable from their main jobs.

Their own immediate managers also disliked it because they had to cope with being unexpectedly short-handed. It's one thing when a planned absence occurs, but to learn only that morning that they would be missing a person was frustrating and inconvenient. We created elaborate emergency rosters for when this happened, but someone always felt it to be unfair, and it probably was.

I learned from this that even though we wanted people to be versatile and helpful, an office does have its own equilibrium and hierarchy, and versatility has its limits. It's one thing to expect someone to pitch in for the good of their department by doing something similar to their regular job: it gets noticed and appreciated by the manager and their team. But pitching in for the good of the office by doing something that is viewed, albeit incorrectly, as relatively menial one, does not always create the same positive results.

In retrospect, we should have done more to elevate the status of the receptionist in the eyes of the staff. As often happens in companies, we did two things that by implication branded the position as inferior. First, we promoted good receptionists out into the operating departments, and second, we sometimes moved people in that role who were not as well suited to the regular business. Ideally, you hire a very good receptionist and pay a very good salary, but managements usually don't like to swell their payroll if they don't absolutely have to, so great receptionists continue to be rare.

While flexibility is important, trying to push work to where it really did not belong was a bad thing—for everyone. Some of the senior people's attitude to the receptionist question was to say "tough," yet if we had tried to drive inappropriate work to them, they would have felt just as aggrieved.

So how did we address the reception issue? After several unsatisfactory solutions, we found the answer in outsourcing. Not only did we outsource the receptionist-relief role, we outsourced all our mailroom and photocopying functions. By hiring a company whose sole business was to execute these kinds of tasks, we got better service, reduced our payroll headcount and eliminated a source of staff frustration.

26

RATIOS

Too much time spent on internal matters is not productive

In corporate America, there is a ratio that reflects the relative amounts of time spent by an operation on (1) internal corporate and political issues and (2) taking care of customers and the business. The greater the amount of time spent on internal matters at the expense of time devoted to the customers, the less successful is that operation. It is usual, though not inevitable, that the larger the corporate organization, the greater will be the time spent on internal issues.

This is one of the pitfalls of any company, that people get so immersed in processes, politics and reorganizations that they become distracted from the core business activities. For the boss, there are two things to learn from this. The first is that you should aim to keep that ratio as high as possible in favor of taking care of business and customers. That means minimizing the internal demands on your staff, such as keeping meetings short and only having them when really needed. Do all you can to keep people focused on what makes money for the company; a busy staff will not have time for internal distractions.

Second, as the boss, you run the risk of having your own personal ratio become overloaded with internal questions. It's easy for this to happen: Performance reviews, corporate matters and systems problems are all necessary internal issues that have to be addressed, but many bosses spend almost all their time on these things, and so could you if you are not careful.

Of course, many bosses hide behind this "work" as a way to avoid outside contact and all the problems that brings. You should recognize this danger and make a big effort to stay in touch with key customers and still get involved in client problems. Don't turn your back on the core business of your operation because you are too busy being boss.

27

GETTING PERSONAL

Addressing employee's personal problems

After you take over as boss, and if you have any kind of paternal or maternal instinct for the people now reporting to you, the issue of personal matters will soon appear. By personal matters I mean non-business topics of any kind. These would include, but certainly not be limited to, spousal, child and other family issues, problems with the house, the car and so on.

Many employees keep this part of their life private and separate from their work life. For them, anything they reveal publicly will usually be positive, such as, "My son's team won the district championship in hockey/baseball/soccer/basketball/ wrestling," and they will share these successes with everyone.

The issue in this chapter is not the good news but the problem news. Now that you are boss, you will find that a few people will frequently gravitate to you bearing gloomy tales from their domestic life. Nothing is too trivial for these people to mention: the carpet installer who did not show up, the leaking roof, the husband with poor health. For some people, that is just how they are, but some may actually use it to gain more time with you, thinking it might give them an advantage.

As a new boss looking for a dialog with your employees, you

might initially encourage these personal discussions, partly because you are somewhat concerned about their problems, partly because you are flattered that they seek your confidence, and partly because you do not want to seem heartless.

While this might be acceptable for your "honeymoon" period, ultimately you should be discriminating about what personal matters you listen to. First, you just don't have the time for it. It is usually irrelevant to the business, and an hour spent in sympathetic listening is an hour that could have been spent on something better. Second, everyone else knows when the office grumbler is sucking up to the boss. If it happens too often, it tends to erode the respect that the others have for you, not just because you are wasting time, but that you are seen as too dumb to realize what's happening.

There is someone you should listen to, and that is your assistant. Because this person works directly with you, it is understandable that you provide a sympathetic ear for her troubles. Some assistants will avail themselves of this privilege more than others. How much time you spend at this is your decision; everyone assumes that you will spend a lot of time with your assistant, and everyone also assumes your assistant is privy to your secrets.

Another exception is what the human resource professionals call "life-changing events" involving really serious problems, such as severe family illness or maybe a spouse's loss of job. When you learn of something truly critical happening in an employee's life, it is usually appropriate to offer your time and any help that they need. The rest of the staff will usually know what is happening and the time you spend helping will be both understood and respected.

28

IN SEARCH OF QUALITY

Avoiding the Quality Trap

Corporate America's commitment to Quality is no longer as fashionable as it was in the 1990s, which generally speaking should be cause for some regret. It's a good thing to try to improve your products and services, and if you are a diligent boss you'll always be trying to improve the performance of your operation, regardless of whether it's the current trend.

But don't fall into the Quality trap. The Quality trap is to exhort your colleagues to do Quality work, to become a Quality operation, to provide Quality service, in fact to use the word Quality at all. It's a trap because striving for Quality is an unattainable goal. Quality is subjective and is therefore interpreted differently by different people, notably your customers. It is aiming for a target that cannot be defined. Quality service for one customer might be just average to another, and this can become especially complicated if your biggest customer is the one most easily pleased.

The Quality trap is striving to achieve something that you cannot measure, and so you never know what progress you are making towards it and you never know when you've achieved it. A mistake companies made in the 1990s was to first elevate

Quality to be the corporate goal and then try to find ways to define it.

Talking about Quality as a goal in itself blurs the focus of the operation., While being opposed to Quality is heretical, having Quality as the goal can actually make people uncomfortable because no one quite knows what it means.

Quality is what naturally happens when everyone does what they are supposed to do, when they are supposed to do it, in order to meet the specific, measurable goals of the operation. Your job as the boss is to set the goals, both for the group and for each individual, design the plan and implement the strategy, which your staff members then execute under your direction.

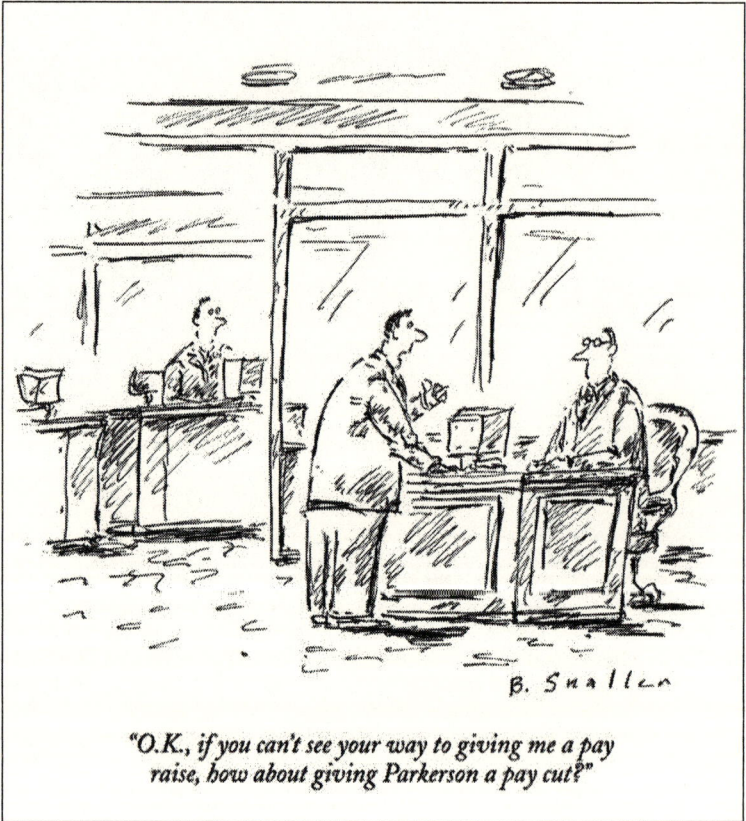

"O.K., if you can't see your way to giving me a pay raise, how about giving Parkerson a pay cut?"

29

MONEY

> Money's easy to make if it's money you want.
> —JOHN STEINBECK, *EAST OF EDEN*

The subject of pay

Compensation will always be fundamental to the employer/
employee contract. But just how important is it in the job
environment? Certainly, most people work because they have to,
but while money may be the reason people go to work, once
there, the situation is a little more complex. Here are five points
to bear in mind on this sensitive subject:

(1) However much you earn, there will always be someone
who earns more. If you earn $30,000, someone is earning
$50,000. If you earn $100,000, someone else is getting
$200,000. You make a million dollars a year? Well, these
days you won't have to look far to find people making
over a million a year. If all you do is wish you were at a
higher salary level, you will be unhappy because there is
always another level. To avoid this particular misery, don't
focus on what other people are getting, but focus instead

on whether what you are getting is appropriate. Are you being fairly paid, relative to what you do, how long you have done it, and how well you do it? These are questions for you, but also points you should consider when reviewing how much you pay your staff.

(2) There are always salary inequities in any organization. Some of this may be the result of biased and unfair management decisions, but often inequities are unavoidable. To bring people in from outside, you often have to pay a little more to attract them. Is this completely fair to the existing, loyal staff? Probably not, yet it is a fact of corporate life. Sometimes a person is paid more relative to his contribution just because he has been there a long time— another almost unavoidable fact of life. If you become the boss of a group of people you are familiar with, you will almost certainly get a surprise when you first see their salaries. Before you start on a mission to create fairness— not necessarily a bad goal—bear in mind that it will take longer than you want, and that it will be almost impossible to achieve. Just when you think you are nearly there, something will happen to create a new imbalance.

(3) For some people, you can never pay them enough. They are usually living above their means and therefore constantly wanting more. These people are not good for the organization. Whatever salary you give them will not be sufficient. Fortunately, they are the most likely to move to another company, in search of a compensation package they will probably never receive.

(4) Unless you rise to the very highest levels, you will probably not get extremely rich working for a corporation. Most employees in corporate America completely understand this fact. They may not like it, but they know it. In the absence of making millions, most of them they just want

to be treated financially appropriately. They know that corporate bonuses are typically not great; they know that not everyone gets one, so a modest, unexpected bonus can produce much gratitude. Staff members know that the average company pay raise is say, four percent. They also have friends in other companies experiencing the same thing, so a raise of seven percent is very welcome.

(5) If all people cared about was money, then everyone would change jobs every couple of years, but of course, they don't. One of the most illuminating incidents I witnessed relating to money concerned the ability of staff to buy or sell a week's vacation. This meant you could take an extra week of vacation but you would not get paid for it. Or, you could "sell back" a week's vacation to the company by working instead of taking the time off. You might think that the lowest-paid employees would want to sell a week to get a little more money; instead most of them took the extra week off and sacrificed that week's pay. They had realized that they would never be rich working in our company. Losing a week's pay was not a critical problem, and although the money they would make from selling a week would be nice, what really mattered was to be able to take some time off to simply spend time with their families.

While money isn't the only thing employees are concerned about, money is still very much an issue at salary review time; you'll always get disagreements and unhappiness. And of course, people do quit their jobs for more money. It may be a fundamental thing, but for most employees, it is by no means the only thing.

30

COCKTAIL PARTY BOSS

Give your full attention as appropriate

You've probably been at a cocktail party and met someone who was more interested in what was going on over your shoulder than in talking you. If so, then you will know how infuriating it is; either give me your full attention or go away, you think.

That is how one of your employees feels when you are supposed to be spending time with them but are willingly diverted by almost anything else that comes along. Some managers like to interrupt meetings or conversations to address something else because they think it makes them look important and smart. Certainly, the ability to focus on a succession of unrelated questions coming at you rapidly is a useful gift, but it's not a good idea to practice this skill during a private talk with a member of staff.

If you have a formal meeting with a colleague in your office, then give that person all of your attention for the duration of the meeting. A focused, five-minute discussion is worth much more than a half hour that's continuously interrupted.

This does not mean you can never be interrupted, but set the rules. If you are waiting for an important call that you must take, then simply tell the person that before you start talking. Make sure your assistant, if you have one, leaves you alone unless it is for a pre-arranged reason—or it's your own boss calling. And if you are not expecting any pressing calls, make sure that your phone is forwarded for someone else to pick up.

If you don't do this and instead want to act like a busy hard-charging executive, you will be perceived to be as rude as that party guest. It is discourteous to be in a meeting and grab the phone as soon as it rings. It's also rude to let your eyes stray to the computer screen to catch any new e-mails that might come in.

Each time you allow your attention to be usurped by an outside source, you send a message that the person you are talking with is of less or even no consequence. That's a bad message to send to an employee.

However, there is a difference between a formal conversation with someone in your office and a casual chat as you are passing through the general workspace. Outside your office the protocols are usually more relaxed. By definition, a chat with an employee as you lean against their cubicle is not at all private and so breaking off to call something out to a passing colleague is not taken badly. As with so much in corporate life, appropriateness is everything.

31

Two Sides

Every issue has more than one perspective

Some day, one of your employees will rush into your office to complain about a fellow worker's conduct. They will forcefully outline exactly what happened, and why the other person is in the wrong, and finally, of course, say that you have to do something about it. Their story will invariably sound plausible, and as you listen you might find yourself being caught up in the apparent injustice of the situation, especially if the complainant is eloquent, and you may even begin to form an idea of how to reprimand the other party.

But however persuasive and believable is the person before you, you should remember that there is always another side to every issue, and both sides must be heard. Before you rush to judgment, get the other side of the story, and get it as soon as possible. When you do this, you might be surprised at how certain things were omitted from the original version that had been edited to show the bearer in as good a light as possible. Note that the second version will also have its own biases, but at least you now have two biased and conflicting versions instead of one biased version.

In a perfect world where you had plenty of time, you might

get a relatively impartial opinion from someone else, but it's likely that you've already spent too long on this, so you should act upon the evidence you have. If it's a repeated conflict between the same characters you might be faced with some tough decisions. It may be that these two will never get along which may mean one or both moving on inside the company or even moving out. Most operations contain people who don't get along yet can normally subdue their feelings enough to do their work, but occasionally these clashes become so significant that action has to be taken.

32

GIVE THEM A BREAK

Your employees are only human

It's Monday morning, and the elevator doors are about to open and you're moments away from starting another week as boss. You are in a particularly good mood: there's things to be done, challenging things, at least in the context of work, and best of all, there are no looming personnel crises that you are aware of. You make your way to your office and as you pass a colleague, you give a friendly "good morning," reflecting your positive mood. But instead of a reciprocal welcome, you get either a mumbled inaudible sound or maybe even silence. Your disposition turns suddenly sour. What is this? You are irked at the impoliteness, even rudeness. You've given a warm greeting, why the tepid response? And so you go to your office, optimism already bruised.

The skill that you need in this situation takes some practice because you feel you have been affronted. You may be the boss, but this small incident should remind you that the people you work with usually live in worlds very different from yours. Just because you feel good does not mean everyone else feels good, however natural it may be to assume this. Your colleague may have had a horrible weekend, perhaps broken up with his girlfriend, and is simply depressed.

Sometimes people just want to be left alone and cannot manage to put on a brave face. (You probably can—and often have to; it's part of being a leader.) But don't expect everyone to have the same ability as you.

There are two things to point out here. First, do not stop saying "good morning" even if it isn't always returned. It makes everyone feel that you're in a good mood and therefore nothing bad is going on or is about to happen. It's infectious: Good habits and politeness rubs off on everyone just as gloom and bad habits rub off, especially from the boss. Second, you must accept the fact that even though you are the boss, and in theory you can go anywhere at any time and demand that people talk to when you require it, your staff do not always want to see you. And it's usually nothing personal. Even if they usually like to see you, there will be times when they either want to be left alone, or are talking to someone else and do not want you as part of the conversation. Learn to recognize this when it happens and don't stick around when you are not welcome.

33

EFFECTIVENESS AND EFFICIENCY

Both are important, but only one is vital

You've probably heard it said at work that "We have got to be more efficient." It sounds reasonable enough: transforming the lumbering vehicle that is your unit, division, subsidiary or company into an efficient machine. Efficiency is a good thing, implying an absence of waste, either of time, effort or materials. But do not confuse efficiency with effectiveness. Achieving efficiencies may be worthwhile, but it is only a means to the real end, which is effectiveness. Efficiency may help you reduce the size of your bills; effectiveness is what pays them.

This is not an original distinction. Management experts at business schools have been stressing it for years. But not every new boss pays close attention to management experts, so it's worth repeating here.

In the mid-1980s, when personal computers with office applications were in their infancy, my company decided to create a customized computer system that would track all the business that came in to our office, who sent it to us, who worked on it and the final outcome. It seems simple enough today, but at that time it involved a huge programming task. After many months, we had a serviceable, if slightly cumbersome computerized business tracking system. My boss and I had spent a lot of time designing the system, and we were very proud of it. Visitors would be escorted over to The Computer (we only had one) and given a demonstration of how efficiently we tracked our business. I was always a bit puzzled why most visitors seemed only politely interested.

It was only years later, after I had learned the difference between efficiency and effectiveness, that I realized why they were not more fascinated: They simply did not care. These visitors were usually our customers, insurance brokers who came to us with hard-to-place insurance programs involving problems and challenges, and as specialty marketers of corporate insurance we would assist them. Consequently, the only thing our customers cared about was whether or not we could solve their problems; Could we provide what they needed, how effective were we? How well we organized and monitored our internal information was of no concern to them. I was boasting about our efficiency, but our customers were only interested in effectiveness. Efficiencies mostly satisfy the internal needs of the operation. That is important, but satisfying the customer (who can be internal as well as external) is what really matters.

34

MEMORANDA

Some basic corporate diplomacy

In business, memos are still the method of choice whenever someone wants to formally pass on an internal message to others. These days they are more likely to be in e-mail format than handed out on paper, but their benefits and drawbacks remain. As a boss, you will use the memo to communicate with your staff, as well as others in the company. Almost by definition, a memo is a management tool, giving information and direction.

Because of the implicit authority of a memo, memos from the least important people in the office are usually not taken seriously and probably for that reason rarely sent. It's one thing for the manager to send a memo to staff requesting that everyone leave their shopping bags in the closet; the same message coming from Sue in the mail room might not have the same impact.

Here are some comments on memos as management tools, beginning with the good things. They are certainly useful for getting basic information and requests to everyone who needs to know. Because of the inherent possibility for containing controversy they tend to get read. They are useful when you are not looking for a debate on an issue, but are using your executive privilege to impose something. They are good for documenting events, which is always helpful six months later when in the absence of a memo no one quite remembers what happened. The use of e-mail for memos has also helped inform far-flung colleagues quickly and simultaneously.

But attractive as memos or e-mails are for the manager, especially the new manager, they carry some liabilities. They should not be used as a substitute for leadership. It's easy to slip into memo-management, hidden away in your office as you send out memo after memo to the unseen and unheard staff, ordering and demanding.

As general rule, try to and put only positive or neutral things in memos. Individual praise should be conveyed in person before being publicized. Bad news should be given personally either in your office or a bigger room, if necessary.

It is rarely good to have bad news in a memo, unless you specifically need it recorded. Accept that when you write a memo it will be read by many people for whom it was not intended, some of whom you would really rather not read it. Take a moment before you fire off a negative memo: would you want your competition to see it? Would you want your boss's boss to see it? What would Human Resources think of it? Would you want your customers to see it? Those people who you don't want to see it invariably get a copy. Even if the negative memo you want to send is accurate, remember that you are not looking for absolute correctness. You're looking to run a successful business operation, and negative memos are usually counterproductive.

If you decide that a memo is the appropriate form of communication for your purpose, almost as important as what you say and when you say it is to whom you send it and who gets a copy. The recipients will be reasonably easy; those who need to get the direct message, but when it comes to the "c.c." group, you have to take into account those who really should see a copy because it is information that they should be aware of, and also those to whom it may not be relevant but who will get upset if they do not get a copy. This tends to apply more to colleagues who are your peers or senior to you; for your junior colleagues this is less important. Use memos carefully; an ill-conceived memo can haunt you for years.

35

NEWTON'S LAW OF MOTION

Every body continues in its state of rest, or of uniform motion in a right line, unless it is compelled to change that state by forces impressed upon it.

—SIR ISAAC NEWTON, 1687

People don't change jobs readily

Sir Isaac Newton's law of motion applies just as much in the workplace as anywhere else. It can be seen on a daily basis, as those colleagues who can't keep still move around the office, gossiping, faxing, running down to the coffee machine, while those bodies who tend not to move around stay at their desk, hopefully working.

However, it is movement on a larger scale that is discussed here, that of movement from job to job. The frequent job-hopper is someone you have probably encountered. Try as they might to shrink them, their resumes are several pages long because there has been so much activity. Generally, there is no reason to hire these people as the chance of them finally finding contentment with your company is remote—a body in motion staying in motion. Conversely, the worker who has been with you for five years will probably stay for five more—a body at rest continuing at rest. What is the point of these observations, and how can it help you as the boss?

It can help because most employees tend to want to stay at rest, and not move jobs every year or two. They usually look for reasons to stick with a company rather than reasons to leave. Certainly, there will be grumbles and complaints, but unless their work environment becomes completely unbearable or they are tempted away by an offer they cannot refuse offer, they will usually choose to remain.

An article in *The New York Times* of August 23, 1998 entitled "The Job Hoppers Have Yet to Conquer" describes how in spite of perceptions, the average job tenure from 1995 to 1997 at mid-size and large companies was 13.4 years, up from 12.6 years during the period 1990 to 1992. A Princeton economist was quoted in the article as saying, "There's just no basis for the idea that the great American job is dead."

And in another survey, this time in Britain during the year 2000, one conclusion was that "The widely assumed picture of a flexible labor market with a growing number of foot-loose employees moving from job to job is far from the truth. There is a good deal more stability in the workplace than is generally supposed."*

The good news for you, at least in the short term, is that this particular management challenge is not too difficult. You don't have to do that much to keep people working with you, or to put it another way, you have to be really bad to force them to look for another job. A desire to support the company and a willingness to put in a fair day's work are actually widespread in the corporate world. Importantly for you, these feelings of corporate loyalty can be triggered relatively easily.

---

*Britain's World of Work—Myths and Realities by Robert Taylor. *Economic and Social Research Council, published June 2003.*

Simply saying thank you or showing verbal appreciation of a good job goes a long way. Conversely, an absence of basic gratitude or appreciation can actually push people into leaving otherwise good jobs. A very senior businessman I know actually left one company and joined another primarily because he had done some great work and no one had bothered to call and thank him for it. Had they done so, he almost certainly would have stayed.

36

TEAMS & PROBLEM SOLVING

Or, the Problem with Teams

Sooner or later in every business organization, someone will talk about teams and teamwork, how important they are, and how things go better when people work in unison. A lot has been written on teams and their value. Catch phrases such as "There's no Me in Team!" highlight the inherent conflict between a successful team and self—interest.

There's a lot of truth in it. Successful teamwork often leads to a successful business operation where there are many tasks that all have to be performed more or less in synchronization.

Effective teamwork can be very powerful. I was at a seminar where the moderator brought out a tray full of maybe thirty different objects, and asked the group to study the objects for only one minute. The tray was removed, and the challenge was to see if any individual could recall all the items. There were no volunteers, so the moderator opened it up to the group. People started calling out objects, and before long all the objects were accounted for as different people remembered different things. What had proved impossible for any one person was accomplished by the group working together.

Well-run teams usually do achieve more than individuals. They demonstrate the basic principle that several minds are better than one, with solutions to problems that are often beyond the reach of most individuals. They can make business more enjoyable and they are good for morale.

So where's the problem? President Harry S. Truman said, "It is amazing what you can accomplish if you do not care who gets the credit." But while there is no doubting the truth of that statement, equally clear is that it is unrealistic.

For in the world of corporate America people care very much who gets the credit and working altruistically as members of a team makes individual recognition that much harder to achieve. The suppression of personal interest for the good of the organization is a noble but rarely attained ideal. "Credit" in the corporate world essentially translates into money. Modestly eschewing credit may be fine for the CEO, but the CEO is almost certainly a rich man. It is not the same for the middle or lower level employees whose monthly living expenses are often barely less than their salaries.

Not caring about who gets the credit is counterintuitive to the survival process going on all day, every day in corporate America. People care who gets the credit because that's how they feel they will be judged and rewarded, and in most cases they are right. Why willingly hide your light under a bushel for the good of the team and risk getting no credit or even worse, risk someone else getting the credit that you deserve?

Teamwork can be very effective, but the manager must understand it's much more complicated than simply selecting various individuals, throwing them together and expecting great things to happen —although there will always be a few employees who unreservedly and unselfishly embrace the team concept. For teams to have a chance of succeeding everyone must understand that they will still get recognition for their contribution to a job done well; the boss must create and maintain incentives for individuals to work together, even if it's nothing more than telling people what a good job they are doing. If people believe it's in their interest and that the purpose is meaningful they can work productively in teams.

"Knock it off, Lewis. Just tell me what's gone wrong."

37

FIX THE PROBLEM, NOT THE BLAME

Hunting for scapegoats is a waste of energy

Mistakes are going to happen in your operation. They happen in every operation, in every business and at every level. You've made mistakes in your career and you'll make more in the future. And so will your employees. Even though it is a cliché, a lot can be learned from mistakes, if you and your colleagues are prepared to learn.

Therefore you should create an environment where mistakes are not automatically punished, so that people are not afraid of admitting to mistakes. Hiding a problem or a mistake only compounds the problems and results in corporate chaos. Things may be so bad that when the mistakes are finally discovered it is you, the boss, who suffers more than the original perpetrators. Mistakes rarely disappear and tend to get worse the longer it takes to reveal them. Encouraging a rapid revelation of mistakes is not only good for the employees and the company; it's ultimately good for you too.

We used to say that the only problem that we could not fix was the one we did not know about. Virtually any business problem internally and externally could be taken care of in some way, even if it sometimes meant a humbling meeting with a client. But a problem can only be fixed if you know about it.

Having made people comfortable with admitting their errors, it's important that all your resources are then devoted to solving the problem and correcting the mistake. To put it succinctly: Fix the problem, not the blame. All too often when something goes wrong, the hunt is on for a scapegoat: "Whose fault is it?" This is counter-productive for not only does it waste your time and energy better spent in putting things right, it helps create the atmosphere you do not want, where people get hounded and punished for errors. Remember that when mistakes do happen, everyone has a pretty good idea of who did it, most of all the unfortunate transgressor. Putting them in an unfavorable spotlight does no one any good; it's rotten for them and sends a bad message to everyone. If you really need to issue a reprimand after the problem has been fixed, do it privately, quietly and constructively; make sure that in discussing the situation you emphasize the "we" have a problem. Avoid using isolating language to infer that "you" have a problem. Talk about what "we" are all going to do to fix it.

Once the crisis is over you and your supervisors should review what happened so you can determine if a larger issue needs to be addressed. But don't spend too long over-analyzing it.

After you have fixed the problem, put it behind you. Don't make the guilty person feel like a pariah, that his career is so damaged he may as well leave. Take pains to show him that the matter is closed, that a lesson was hopefully learned, and that everyone should now move on. It's especially important to perform a public display of encouragement towards the offender, so that everyone else can see no bad feelings linger, and that no one is being ostracized.

While we are talking about problems, it's worth mentioning that just as the best companies are always searching out complaints so they can fix them and create a satisfied customer, the best bosses are always looking for problems they can fix. For these bosses, problems are often welcomed as a way to make the operation better. These bosses are actually happiest when solving problems and often nervous when things appear to be going smoothly.

38

KEEP IT SIMPLE

It's hard to focus on multiple challenges

Here are two stories, both about election campaigns. The first story concerns the 1992 U.S. presidential election. The incumbent, George Bush, was still basking in the glory from a successful Gulf War less than two years earlier and appeared to be the favorite. But the challenger, Bill Clinton, did a very smart thing. He hired a man called James Carville to spearhead his campaign. James Carville and his colleagues did an even smarter thing. They managed to condense their whole campaign into one simple, memorable slogan: "It's the economy, stupid!" Against considerable odds, Clinton won the election.

Just after his election, a cartoon by Jeff MacNelly appeared in the *Chicago Tribune*. It showed Clinton sitting behind his president's desk looking a bit stunned, and behind him pinned to the wall, are a mass of small notes. They are all basically similar but different in the details. Here is a sample of what they said. "It's the Middle East, stupid!" "It's healthcare, stupid!" "It's Russia, stupid!" "It's Northern Ireland, stupid!" "It's Education, stupid!" "It's the environment, stupid!"

It was a good cartoon and a point well made that in 1992 there were many more issues for the president to face than the economy. However stunned Clinton may have looked in MacNelly's drawing, the real Bill Clinton was well aware that all those issues would be waiting for him the morning after his inauguration. What he also knew was that if he had tried to make all those issues part of his campaign, he would not have been elected. There are two reasons for this. First, people might disagree on a solution for the Middle East, or on the best way to protect the environment, but in 1992 most people could agree that the economy was in bad shape.

Second, and of more relevance here, is that people have difficulty focusing on more than one thing a time. We like to believe otherwise, but the reality is that if you want people to keep something in mind, one thing is about all they can really attend to. The entire Clinton election campaign was driven by one idea, put across effectively.

The other story took place during the 2001 United Kingdom general election. In the politically unremarkable district of Kidderminster, the governing Labour party candidate was expected to win reelection.

But in Kidderminster a strange thing happened. Services at the local hospital—Kidderminster Hospital, under the control of the National Health Service—were being drastically cut back. Serious medical cases were being sent to another hospital many miles away. This was causing general unhappiness among the residents of Kidderminster and creating fury in the mind of one of the doctors at the hospital, Dr. Richard Taylor. But rather than fume, he decided to do something, which was to run for election to Parliament. He was a doctor, not a politician, and he was running for only one reason, which was to keep the Kidderminster hospital open. That was his platform, nothing else.

He not only won the election, he won comfortably. Just like the American election campaign of Bill Clinton, he focused on an issue that almost everyone in Kidderminster could agree on, and like Bill Clinton's campaign it was only one issue.

How do these stories relate to the mid-level boss in corporate America? Don't confuse people by sending multiple messages. Don't produce a list of eight bullet points that have to be addressed for the operation to meet its goals. Don't even produce a list of two things: Just produce one.

You can introduce a new bullet point later, after the first has been worked through, but for your bullet points to have any chance of being noticed and acted upon they must be consecutive, not simultaneous. Pick the one thing that you think most needs attention and make that your goal for the operation. If customer service is slipping you might mandate that all calls be returned in twenty-four hours. That's fine; just don't be tempted to add anything else.

Producing multiple challenges is especially common in performance appraisals. The poor employee who hasn't actually done too badly is presented with five key areas in which she is expected to improve. She can't address five things at the same time—she's too busy working, and you can't monitor five different things either. Give her one thing to address that she can focus on and you can monitor. If you really think she needs to address more than one thing, have her work on the first for three months and then introduce a second. If she can't manage to improve the first thing, then you all have a more serious problem.

Some bosses who produce a long list of "things to improve" do so as much for their own benefit as that of the employee so that the review appears meaningful. There is sometimes a corporate directive that says reviews have to contain at least three items to be worked on by the employee. This is nonsense because the boss is then put in the position of trying to find some minor fault to be corrected just for the sake of the review. Inventing issues or conjuring up problems that don't exist is ridiculous, but in the review process it happens the whole time. So don't just keep it simple, keep it very simple.

Many people, after reading this chapter, will still produce

lists containing more than one thing, quietly believing that whatever they might read here, they can certainly manage to cope with at least two. But remember even by listing just two items you have immediately cut in half the amount of time available to work on any single thing, and have set up competing demands. These can then be played off against each other:

"Shall I work on my writing skills this week or shall I work on my poor punctuality?" ponders the employee. And when as boss you review the progress made you'll hear, "I know I've been coming in late but I've been working hard on my writing skills!" What do you do then? Admonish him or praise him? Keep it simple and start with the punctuality and when that's under control address the writing skills.

39

THE SLEDGEHAMMER AND THE WALNUT

Address problems appropriately

People will continually come to the boss with problems, some big some small, some internal some external. I always felt that one of the attractions of being in this position was that I never knew on any day where the problems would be, only that there would almost certainly be something somewhere. If the idea of facing a daily stream of challenges (i.e. problems) does not appeal, then you are probably not suited to be the boss. The point of this chapter will be illustrated by a story that happened in our office several years ago.

We were having our usual bi-weekly managers' meeting when someone brought up an issue concerning our receptionist. Although a relatively small operation of around fifty people, we ran several different businesses. Our receptionist complained that sometimes people called not knowing exactly who to talk to, and she was not familiar enough with all our various operations to know where to direct the call. Could we prepare an overview of all the operations so that she would know how to handle such calls? It sounded reasonable, and the discussion moved off into how much space we should devote to each description, who should organize it and so on. It was the conventional, corporate analysis of the problem.

At this point, luckily, one of my wiser colleagues asked the question, "How often does the receptionist get put in this position?" We had no idea, so someone slipped out from the conference room to ask her directly. Back came the response, "about two or three times a year." We instantly agreed that it was not worth investing the time and effort to deal with it. She would have to handle with these few queries as best she could, without the time-consuming document she wanted.

We were close to making a common business error—using a sledgehammer of a solution to crack a walnut of a problem. Not every problem is worth spending time to fix. When you are a new boss, it's easy to get waylaid by people looking to eat up your time with trivial issues. You will probably feel you have to give them your full attention. That's fine for a while, but you should learn to apportion your time and efforts appropriately. As the boss, you have a sledgehammer; use it to attack the big problems, not the small ones, and remember that not every problem is even worth addressing.

40

THE SUGGESTION BOX

Make sure you know what people really want

During one of our managers' meetings, someone brought up the idea of a Suggestion Box. This idea had originated from general comments by the staff. We discussed it and all agreed that it was probably not a bad idea and would give everyone a chance to offer constructive suggestions under the cloak of relative anonymity, if that was what they wanted. I added the usual condition that while all the suggestions would be reviewed and discussed, I reserved the right not to implement them. So we looked in the office supply catalog, and there we found a beautiful wooden Suggestion Box, with a shiny brass plate, announcing something like "Suggestions Here," just below a small mail slot. It also came with a supply of suggestion cards, nicely printed, with a place for the suggestion, and a place for the "suggesters" to write their name (this was optional).

We ordered it that day. When it arrived a week or so later, around went a memo saying we had bought it, where it would be located and how we looked forward to getting suggestions that would help propel our company forward. Each day for about a week I unlocked the box, and each day it was empty. After a couple of weeks, we did get something: "I suggest we close the office at lunchtime on Fridays to let everyone enjoy the summer." Not too helpful for a service company.

That was the last suggestion we received, and after a few more weeks I stopped looking in the Box. What happened? How did the seemingly popular demand for a Suggestion Box fizzle out? At first I put it down to corporate inertia, but I eventually came to realize what had happened; people did not want to actually make formal suggestions, what they wanted was a Suggestion Box. They wanted to have the vehicle to make suggestions, to have the outlet for suggestions, and once they got it they did not care whether they used it or not.

This taught me an important lesson, which was to recognize the difference between what people said they wanted and what they really wanted. People are always doing things for reasons not immediately apparent. Do people eat at restaurants just because they are hungry? An article in the *New York Times* of February 3, 1998, quotes a waiter as pointing out that "many people are at a restaurant because they want recognition, attention, or simply to belong to something." No mention of hunger there. It helped teach me something else, which was that while everyone has an *opinion* on everything that does not mean they *care* about everything.

The challenge for the boss is to discern the difference between what the employees say they want or appear to want, and what they really want: Is it just opinion, which is cheap, or do they really care? Do they really want to make suggestions or do they just want a Suggestion Box?

It is interesting (and frustrating) that in the workplace, the feedback you get from people reporting to you is often inversely related to your desire for it. If you float an idea and specifically look for comments, it is likely that the usual minority will let you know what they think but the usual silent majority will remain so. However, if you decide to make a unilateral decision without seeking input or opinion, the feedback you receive is often substantial. When you really want feedback you'll get little; when you really don't want it, you'll probably get a lot.

People want the opportunity to give their comments; actually giving them is of less interest. Giving feedback when none is asked for is partly a protest against the lack of opportunity to respond. It is also because people are fickle; you can't change this so you should at least recognize it.

Postscript

Even though this chapter is not really about Suggestion Boxes, they are still a feature of corporate America. An accurate appraisal of them comes from Herb Kelleher, founder of Southwest Airlines and one of the preeminent leaders and managers.

> "We tell people that if you need a suggestion box, then you're not doing what you should be doing. You shouldn't have to interpose the box between yourself and the people with the ideas. You ought to be talking to them on a regular basis. You ought to be with your people enough that they are comfortable to just pop on in and give you their ideas."
>
> —*FORTUNE* Magazine, May 28, 2001

41

FUN?

You can't force fun

Back in the mid-1990s, company mission statements were very popular. Not a bad idea, because in creating them people actually had to think about what their company was supposed to be doing. However, soon most companies had a mission statement, and of course, if everyone has one and they all look pretty much alike—which they did—then it's almost the same as no company having one.

Occasionally, you would come across a mission statement that displayed all the usual verbs, phrases and adjectives (strive, be the best we can be, superior service, excellence) but there would be a small section about having fun while doing all these noble things. On the surface it didn't seem too outrageous a goal: why not aim to have some fun? But just as governments have found that they cannot mandate happiness in their citizens, a company cannot really have "fun" as an objective and specifically try to create it.

Work is work. It's not a place that's built for fun. Work is challenging, to say the least. While you are there, you try to do your job as best you can, and hope that you get some personal satisfaction from its successful execution, as well as a fair salary.

Any fun you might have at work is incidental and collected along the way. It's a bit like frequent-flyer miles from an airline: They usually are not the reason you took the trip but it's nice to get them. If something fun happens, well that's great and it is a pleasant bonus, but it needs to happen by itself without any corporate prodding.

What has this got to do with being the boss? Even though you can't just order up some fun like you order paper clips, you can be instrumental in creating a work environment where "fun" has at least a chance of breaking out. Is your workplace somewhere that your staff dread coming to each day because of your behavior, or is it a place where they actually don't mind spending a large part of their day? Is it a place where their good work will be recognized, their bad work will be corrected without necessarily dooming their career, where they will learn, where they feel the opportunities are reasonably equal and where their voice can be heard? And where, from time to time, they might even have a little fun on the side? As the boss, you really do have the ability to create this environment. Fun can certainly break out in spite of a miserable workplace, but it's far more likely to happen where the situation is favorable because of your influence.

Fun stands a better chance if your operation retains a sense of balance. Work is basically a serious place, but in corporate America it's rarely a matter of life and death. There will be times when, in spite of everyone's best efforts, everything seems to be going wrong; clients are angry, systems are malfunctioning and suppliers are letting you down. When this happens, it is a short step from tragedy to farce and you should try to recognize the black humor inherent in the situation. It's not good when this happens, but things will almost certainly get better—as you must keep telling everyone!

42

MEETINGS

Handle with care

I have a friend who likes to organize games of touch football on Sunday mornings in the fall. My friend is good at touch football, and loves to play it. I, however, am not good at touch football, so when the call comes from my friend to show up for a game of touch football, I politely declined.

I, on the other hand, am better at soccer. If my friend were to organize a Sunday morning soccer game, I would probably show up. But my friend will never organize a soccer game because he is not very good at soccer. He only likes to do those things that he can do well. In this he is not so very different from me and my preference for soccer, nor so very different from most other people.

What has this got to do with meetings? In business, meetings are everywhere and all the time. The bigger the organization, typically the more meetings there are. In small organizations everyone is usually too busy to have meetings. Some meetings are necessary, but fewer is usually better.

However, not everyone performs well in meetings; those who do perform well like to have meetings. They like to demonstrate how articulate they are; they like to make their voices heard. Just like my friend who loves touch football, they like meetings because they are good at them.

But those who do not perform well in meetings dread them. They dislike witnessing the strong performance of others, a discomfort compounded by their own weak showing.

A lively meeting with a frank and thoughtful exchange of views is the corporate ideal but it can also be a corporate myth. In reality, the same few individuals dominate all the meetings and the silent majority will say little or nothing. Without strong leadership, decisions are rarely made and often postponed, leading to yet further meetings.

As the boss, you must recognize the limitations of meetings. Being quiet in a meeting does not mean someone has nothing to say, so you must give the employees an appropriate opportunity to express themselves.

I have read that in Japan, meetings serve a different function. Instead of a forum to openly discuss unresolved issues, meetings are simply the vehicle by which a decision that has already been agreed upon is communicated and ratified. The actual discussion and debate take place in private sessions, often between just two people—the meeting being the formal presentation of the conclusions. This process in Japanese is called *nemawashi*.

I used to think that this was a bit odd, but now I see the advantages. Many of the awkward dynamics present in typical meetings are removed, such as people's reluctance to openly disagree or contradict someone in public. Also, if proposals are being heard for the first time, it's often hard to properly assimilate them and immediately comment constructively.

In conventional "Western" meetings, the success of a proposal can depend as much on the effectiveness of the presentation as the merit of the idea itself. This means a badly presented but good idea can get sidelined, while an ill-conceived plan advocated forcefully can get accepted. This, of course, is crazy; *nemawashi* removes many of these problems by analyzing issues away from the glare of the meeting room. You can't avoid meetings: Understand their drawbacks, and give some thought to the benefits of *nemawashi.*

43

HUMAN RESOURCES

You will regularly need their help

Years ago, what is now known as Human Resources was called simply the Personnel Department. Those who worked in it would typically be involved when people either joined the company or left the company. In between those events, the Personnel staff would seldom be visible. That has all changed. Today's Human Resources department is still involved when employees come and go, but it now plays a more important role in the operation of the company.

In addition to when people come and go, managers are confronted everyday with a daunting array of federal government measures designed to protect the interests of the employees. These are the law and so adhering to them is not optional. Here are some of the more frequently encountered laws that you must be aware of: Family Leave and Medical Leave Act 1993; Older Worker Benefit Protection Act 1990; Civil Rights Act 1991; American Disabilities Act 1993.

Note that the oldest of these laws has only been enacted for just over a decade, reflecting the increased importance of legislation in the work place. It also means a greater level of corporate and managerial care is needed to be in compliance. As a new boss, you will not be expected to know these statutes in detail, but you will be expected to know about them in general, and you will certainly be expected to consult the Human Resources department whenever you face a situation where such legislation might be involved.

Not coincidentally, also in the last ten years, there has emerged a new kind of insurance for companies called Employment Practices Liability. This insurance protects companies that have been accused by their employees of acts of discrimination, abuse or harassment, often specifically related to an employer allegedly violating one of these statutes. Thousands of employment practice lawsuits are filed by disgruntled employees every year, and have cost companies millions of dollars.

For a young executive rising through the company, few things can derail a career more than being the object of an employment practices lawsuit. At best, it costs the company money and time; at worst, the case may become newsworthy and then it may cost the company its reputation. For a manager, being ignorant of these risks is unacceptable. You may not ever need Human Resources to help with your clients, but you will definitely need their help with your internal employee matters.

It is important that soon after your promotion, you make a point of getting to know the staff in Human Resources, and stay on good terms with them.

"And another thing, Beckton, I don't recall ever saying, 'Correct me if I'm wrong.'"

44

BETTER THAN YOU?

Appreciate the various talents in your operation

We have seen that as a new boss, you may be feeling very confident in your abilities. This is understandable and a not a bad thing. You've achieved one of the few visible marks of recognition in corporate America. It might be tempting to think that you are also the best employee in your operation, but that would be a mistake.

In most corporate settings, there are many different challenges: customers and clients, suppliers and vendors, internal personnel issues, diplomacy issues, technical skill issues, internal politics. It is unlikely that you are the best person at each of the skills that is required for a successful operation. Using a symphony orchestra as a metaphor, the conductor is not the best oboe player in the orchestra or the best violin player or maybe not the best at any of the instruments, but it is the conductor who sets the tone and the pace and gets everyone in tune and in time.

At work, recognize that Alec is better than you at working with your largest customer; admit that your technical grasp will never be up to Mary's; concede that Sam gets deals from the suppliers that you probably couldn't. And when you have recognized this, be grateful that you are indeed surrounded by experts in their particular specialties and that their skills make the operation a success and make you look good.

Be sure you let people know you respect their skill and never attempt to downplay these skills. Don't say that Alec just happens to get on with his customers as if it were pure chance. Alec works hard at it, and acknowledging this privately to him and publicly to his colleagues is one of the most mature and admired things you can do as a leader. Don't devalue Mary because she pores over the data and details and as a result knows your products better than anyone else. These are people you want working with you. Your challenge is to bring all their skills together, not to vie with them for supremacy in their particular specialty.

Less comforting is the possibility that there may be someone among your staff who is better equipped to be the boss than you are. In corporate America, where pure merit is just another way to get ahead, this is not unusual. After one of my former companies was acquired, I reported to a new boss. Out of the six people who reported to her, all but one would have been a better boss than the one we actually had. If you do recognize a real leader among your employees, the worst thing you can do is suppress their talent and their progress.

What you should do is treat this as a great opportunity to have your replacement ready so you can be moved on to bigger things. By lining someone up in this way, you will probably find your own advancement is actually accelerated, because you've already solved one part of the puzzle for your own senior management. Highlighting someone who might replace you will do you more good than suppressing them. There is another good reason to help these rising stars as much as you can: You may be reporting to them one day.

45

TECHNOLOGY

New machines will not fix people problems

Before voicemail, unanswered ringing telephones were eventually picked up either by a co-worker tired of the noise, a secretary if you were lucky, or bounced back to the switchboard. Whoever eventually handled the call would usually transcribe the message on a pink phone call message pad and this message would then be passed to the recipient.

On one level it worked fairly well. In an office full of busy people, calls seldom got to the intended person the first time, so these pink message notes would pile up. Part of the ritual of office life was to sift through your pile, assigning importance, and then return the calls. Those less diligent workers would let their pile grow, putting off the unpleasant calls. A sign of a bad worker was to see piles of these pink notes on their desk, clearly unanswered.

In the post-voicemail era, most people leave such detailed messages that you don't have to return the call just to find out what the caller wants. Whole transactions can take place without the two parties actually speaking to each other. There is also the miracle of e-mail, which amounts to having your own sophisticated telex machine at your desk. There are also paging devices. formerly the mark of some status, pagers are now universal. And of course, almost everyone has a portable phone.

This is a powerful battery of technology tools to let everyone keep in touch at all times. But however sophisticated the tools become, you should understand that while technology can help a good worker become even more productive, technology will never make a bad worker good. Someone who put off returning the pink message calls will not return the voicemail, the e-mail, or the page.

Don't make the mistake of throwing technological aids at mediocre employees, thinking you will turn them into great employees. Don't pretend that not having the right equipment is holding back chronic under-performers. Don't put off making an unpleasant management decision while you provide better and more costly equipment; that is not where the problem usually lies.

46

SOUNDS REASONABLE?

Logic does not always prevail

It's a fair assumption that throughout your career you have tried to take a rational, thought-out approach to most issues that you have encountered. Corporations generally approve of this approach to business, and so does society.

But in your new management role, you are about to encounter a perplexing and frustrating phenomenon. One of your employees is resisting an idea or a suggestion, and as far as you can see, he is making no sense: "Why can't he understand what is going on?" you ask yourself. What I realize now—but didn't always—is that it is very hard or even impossible to reason someone out of a position that they did not reason themselves into in the first place. If someone thinks through a problem rationally, it is usually not too hard for them to change their mind if there is new evidence or changed circumstances. This is partly because a true reasoning process is an impersonal process in which they have no particular personal stake.

But if someone takes a position based on feelings, bias, prejudice, or personal taste, then you will be unlikely to move them. Think of sports allegiances. If someone supports the Boston Red Sox, they tend to support them however badly they play. They may criticize the team and they may not go to see them very much, but it is unlikely that "rational" factors such as having a bad year or hot-dog prices increasing up will cause the fan to switch his allegiance to another team. In sports, people realize this. Would you try to persuade this fan that he should change teams and support the New York Yankees? No. He almost certainly did not reason himself into following the Red Sox, and you are not going to reason him out of it.

In 1957, a man called Albert Szent-Gyorgi wrote that "The human brain is not an organ of thinking but an organ of survival, like claws and fangs." Szent-Gyorgi was a Nobel prizewinner in biochemistry. The brain, he went on to say, "is made in such a way as to accept as truth that which is only advantage." *

Once you read those words much of what you see in the work place that appears irrational becomes a little clearer. The larger the corporation, the clearer it becomes. If a worker has to choose between a rational decision and one that is less sensible but which strengthens his survival chances, it is rare that the rational option is taken.

Most people in business will tend to do only that which produces benefit to them. Devotion to survival and self-interest rather than doing what is best for the business is an underlying cause of dysfunction in American corporate life. Your own staff will demonstrate this principle on a regular basis, and you will almost certainly do the same whenever you agree with your own boss's pet idea that privately you feel makes no sense.

---

* I would like to acknowledge an article by Michael Schrage in *Fortune* magazine, January 21, 2002, which introduced me to Albert Szent-Gyorgi.

47

PRAISE

Our praises are our wages.

—WILLIAM SHAKESPEARE, *THE WINTER'S TALE (ACT 1, SCENE II)*

Always give praise when it's due

Everyone likes being praised. Some clearly like it, some people might pretend they don't need it, but whether it's the CEO or the mailroom clerk, they all welcome it. I have read that some people do not have to be praised, that they can "praise themselves," and that's sufficient. I don't agree with that; wherever it's due, the boss should give praise.

Don't devalue praise by inappropriate overuse, but if in doubt err on the side of giving it. It costs neither you nor the company anything, although you might think otherwise from the parsimonious way it is parceled out at most companies.

Sometimes, a scarcity of praise can have unexpected results. One of my most effective colleagues was someone who worked long hours every day, but did not shrink from telling me at every opportunity how hard he was working. He was good at his job, and some of the long hours were justified, but I felt that he was spending more time than he had to at work, and I was slightly irritated at the way he always emphasized his long hours. So when

I asked how things were going, and his reply included a reference to how, "Don didn't call me back till after seven o'clock!" I either ignored the comment, or made some flippant remark about how lazy Don was.

He never seemed to get the hint. But looking back, I realize that stressing his work habits was a plea for praise. Unfortunately, the more he said how hard he worked, the more resolute I was in avoiding the issue. Why would he need praise? He made a good salary, we rewarded him with bonuses and promotions, it did not occur to me to take some time to say what a great job he was doing and how much we appreciated his efforts. Had I done this, I'm sure his griping would have been reduced; he would have got what he was really looking for. It was me who did not get the hint.

I should have remembered how grateful I was for the rare words of praise from my own boss, but I never made the connection between liking the little praise I got and how important it was that I praise others.

Bosses themselves need praise because they typically get so little of it. Praising your own boss smacks of sucking-up to most people, (and you should watch out for sycophantic employees during your first months as a new boss). So who is going to praise the CEO? Other CEOs? Doubtful. The board of directors can, but mostly in a formal setting. The stock analysts might, if warranted, and the shareholders might, if something special has happened. But it's not just lonely being at the top, there are not many pats on the back. Of course, you might argue that being paid $1,000,000 a year plus a bonus, generous stock options and benefits makes up for a lot of pats, and you might be right.

48

CELEBRATION TIME

Celebrate success

When I first became a boss, my philosophy was based on taking an unemotional, even-handed approach to triumphs and problems. I never liked it when bosses became enraged over work problems. Losing their temper never seemed to help, it just made everyone upset. People who attacked problems with a calm but resolute purpose always seemed to do best.

I took the same approach to success as I did to problems. No wild enthusiastic celebrations, no whooping, no bell ringing. Balance was everything. Good news today might be bad tomorrow, so let's not get too excited. I might have been right on the bad news: panic and yelling do not help when there is a problem, but I was mostly wrong on how to celebrate good news. People enjoy celebrating, and in an office environment celebration has important other elements beyond simple pleasure.

There is a strong cathartic quality: "We've worked hard and now it's time to release the tension." There is a vindication quality: "We got what we worked for and our efforts have been justified." There is an endorsement quality: "What we did was a good thing in the eyes of the company, which means my future is a bit brighter." Finally, the approval quality: "The boss liked what we achieved."

We have seen how your staff will take its lead from you, your clothes and your habits. They will also take their attitude to success from you, and if you act like success is no big deal, just business as usual, then soon they'll be the same, which is not what you want. If success or failure become barely distinguishable and you act the same whether it's good news or bad, then what's so special about the good?

Consequently, people will not strive quite so hard for success, because it gains no special recognition from the boss. That is bad news for your operation. You need a culture where people are thrilled when they succeed and the company is thrilled with them. You may be secretly elated, but unless you demonstrate it how are your colleagues going to know? They can't read your mind!

You have to be calm in crises, but be thrilled with success. If you elevate its importance, so will your staff. It clearly makes you happy and they like anything that makes you happy. And of course, celebrating success is a lot of fun; it's enjoyable. When things are going bad, it's hard to find the right things to say; when things go well there are lots of things to say and lots of good things you can do.

Postscript

If you decide that the celebration of a great success should involve your support staff, make sure that you go where they want to go, and not where you want to go or think they might want to go. You will probably have acquired a sophisticated palate, courtesy of many expense account dinners, and for the office celebration you think you might want to try that new bistro you've heard about. However, your support staff has not had the benefit of scores of free meals at expensive restaurants, and it's almost certain that their idea of a lunchtime treat is a lot different from yours. So ask them where they want to go, and take them there.

49

A LITTLE INSURANCE

More corporate diplomacy

You may now be the boss, but unless you are the CEO, it's likely that you still have a boss or two of your own. This means that while they expect you to take care of your operation—especially take care of all the humdrum tasks for which middle management partly exists—you do not have complete freedom to do whatever you want. There will be issues that impact other units or departments, issues that affect the firm's image to the outside world, or even purely internal departmental issues that are especially sensitive.

When these situations arise, you would be well advised to take out some personal career insurance. This means alerting your boss to the particulars of the situation, telling him what you have in mind, and making sure it's acceptable. If you plough ahead with your decision without informing him, it's likely that one of his first thoughts on learning about it will be, "I wish I'd have known she was going to do that!" It may irritate him enough into actually saying, "I wish you had told me first."

Two things are happening here. One is the perversity of human nature. Had you told him first, he would probably have said "Fine, go ahead." Second, no one in business likes surprises, and by not telling him yourself, he will probably learn of your decision from elsewhere. First, this embarrasses him as well as surprising him. It gives the appearance he did not know what was happening in his part of the universe. Embarrassing your boss in a business context is a serious mistake. Most bosses hate to be embarrassed.

Second, it means he heard about it through someone else's interpretation rather than yours. In corporate America, this is never a good thing, because the chances of any third party's interpretation being beneficial to you are slim. Telling him ahead also gives him time to prepare his responses to the world, as well as some "ownership" in the decision that will make him more ready to defend it.

Therefore, give him appropriate warning, and always have a proposed solution ready for when you present the problem. Avoid making him do the work. It's much easier for him to critique your idea than to come up with one himself. If you ask his opinion often enough without having a suggested solution ready, he'll start to wonder why you are even there.

Note that it's almost as important to warn your boss about good news. This is, of course, a more pleasant duty, but the effect of him hearing about your good news from someone other than you can be just as embarrassing as it is for bad news. It makes him look equally out of touch. This is important because some people might be modestly inclined not to boast about a success, but those feelings are irrelevant and should be put aside. The glow of success will be quickly clouded if your boss is irritated because you didn't tell him first. In business, there is really no such thing as a good surprise.

50

APOLLO 13

Don't argue about the difficulties.
The difficulties will argue for themselves.

—WINSTON CHURCHILL

You need solutions, not excuses

Even before you became the boss, you knew what the obstacles were that lay between the operation and success. Now that you are the boss, you have probably discovered a few more reasons why achieving those quarterly, semi-annually and yearly goals seems an insurmountable task. Moreover, while previously you were just responsible for your own success, which you could largely control, you are now responsible for the whole operation, which is much harder to control. In fact, it's probably causing you panic attacks as you survey the scene and realize your fortune is now largely in the hands of others, and you will be judged on their ability to perform, not just your own.

If those obstacles to success don't appear to be going away, you will start to hear some things you know only too well—an explanation why targets are not being met. A few colleagues will be able to recite in detail all the reasons for the failure to achieve the goals. It may be realistic defeatism, but it's still defeatism.

Are they wrong? Not completely. The difficulties are real enough, but how you react to people proclaiming these seemingly undeniable truths is critical to your role as leader.

If you've seen the movie *Apollo 13*, you'll recall there is one scene where a filter in the stricken spacecraft is not working, and the air quality is rapidly getting worse. It is a potentially fatal problem. Needing a solution, the team back on the ground puts a bunch of engineers in a room and throws on the table replicas of everything that the astronauts have with them: duct tape, boxes, tubes, and so on.

It looks like a pile of garbage, which is essentially what it is. The instruction to the engineers was simple: Fix the problem using what you see before you. How many reasons were there for the engineers to say it could not be done? That, however, was not an acceptable response; Mission Control was not looking for a list of excuses. Of course, it was difficult but they needed solutions, which they got. Out of that pile of debris the engineers fashioned a filter, relayed instructions to the crew who implemented the solution and fixed the problem.

The workplace is a less dramatic location, but your response as the leader must be the same: Don't tell me why it can't be done, tell me how you are going to do it, make sure you ask for help if you think you need it, and when it's done tell me how you succeeded. We all know it's tough. So how do we overcome it? We need reasons why we can do it, not excuses why it can't be done. If you get too many of the latter, perhaps it's time to reevaluate some of your staff.

"*Keep up the good work, whatever it is, whoever you are.*"

51

DETAILS

Being boss does not mean ignoring details

Once they have achieved a management position, some bosses feel they are now "big picture" people, away from the daily grind of details and processes. While it is very important to keep a leader's perspective, it is just as crucial you not lose sight of the details, and that you maintain a willingness to get involved with the details when the situation demands it.

The very best managers know that every successful enterprise, however big, is simply an aggregation of many small tasks that have to be performed well. Sam Walton, the founder of Wal-Mart, recognized that his huge company was the sum of its individual stores, and if individual stores were not performing, then ultimately neither would the company. That's why he used to show up unannounced at his stores, to see what was going on firsthand. If you follow a successful boss around her operation, you will see her constantly checking to see if things are running as they should.

Apart from being a necessary part of a manager's job, attention and respect for details will win respect from the employees. Their jobs are mostly in the details: If you appear not to care about the details, why should they?

A possible danger of getting immersed in the details of day-to-day operations is that a manager may find refuge there. This is particularly true if the manager was promoted from within the department and is moving from a role in which she was both comfortable and successful into a position that is unfamiliar and challenging. Drifting back into her former habits can be appealing, especially when there are some difficult managerial issues to be faced: "Sorry, Andy, we'll have to put off our meeting about your internal transfer request—I'm really tied up with Sally on the Amalgamated account . . ."

I can't think of a business where the details are not important; I can however think of many businesses where details are not merely important, they are everything. Can the conductor of a professional orchestra allow some musicians to play a little off-tempo? Can a brain surgeon get by with being "close enough?" Or can an aircraft maker overlook a few loose screws? Let's put it another way: If your operation made aircraft, would you fly in one?

52

LOVE AMONG THE CREDENZAS

Inevitable office affairs

It is likely that you will find yourself having to deal with an office affair. Most companies have their own particular rules on this that can range from zero tolerance to benign acceptance. Simply putting humans close to each other is often cause enough for affairs to develop, but to help explain how these things progress, it is important to understand that an office environment is an especially nurturing one.

First, everyone is looking or at least trying to look their best when they are at work. They are usually on their best behavior, they are trying to look poised and business-like, they are trying to act and speak intelligently, and sometimes they actually pull it off. And they all spend so much time together. Continual interaction can be unwelcome if people do not get along, but when there is a spark of attraction eight or ten hours a day of intermittent contact for the parties involved is wonderful.

To help expedite the affair, alcohol usually plays a part with drinks after work. It's a dangerous mix for a group of people who at any time may be single and looking for love, or not single and still looking for love.

Whatever anyone tells you, affairs in the office are a bad thing. Once an affair becomes public knowledge, no one is more anxious to calm your fears than the individuals involved, who will reassure you that everything will be just fine, and that they'll keep their personal life quite separate. But, of course, they say this when everything is going well and they don't dream that there will ever be any discord between them. It's also a selfish position: While they may declare that nothing will change in the office, they can only speak for themselves. It does not take into consideration the impact on everyone else. The reality is that office affairs introduce a factor that can throw the whole operation off balance. Constructive criticism and comments have to be amended, the specter of favoritism appears, and a lot of time gets wasted as everyone discusses it.

Don't fool yourself into believing that everything will be fine, that as long as you don't actually catch them in a passionate clinch or a fistfight you can probably handle it. In this case, your own concerns are the very least of your problems. The affair may be of little consequence in your own career, after all you're already the boss, but for the rest of your staff, it can be a huge issue. You might hear nothing directly negative about it, but that's an illusion; the fact that no one is commenting adversely is a sign that people are just being careful.

If it's a senior, successful professional involved with a junior assistant, then all the peers of the professional will say nothing bad because they feel the success of that person gives him a strong standing both with you and in the company, so by objecting they risk alienating a powerful colleague. Their own dealings with the junior half of the couple will also be compromised. If she does poor work, they will feel less willing to criticize her. As for the peers of the junior woman, they will feel, often with justification, that she will get preferential treatment.

And that's when things are going well. When the romance

runs into trouble, the whole office is tiptoeing around, dreading that they might be caught up in the crossfire and fearing embarrassing situations. All those promises about keeping work and private life separate vanish as the two parties pout and sulk their way around the office. Should the romance end, the impact can be enormous.

Productive work is hard for everyone in these circumstances. If the relationship is serious, then the only lasting solution is for one of them to leave their job and either find a new, unrelated assignment within the firm, or join another company. This solution sounds hard and it is. (You must also make sure you that you check with Human Resources about any legal implications.) From the boss's perspective, there is almost nothing good about affairs in the office.

53

MANAGE THE BUSINESS; LEAD THE PEOPLE

A critical distinction

Bosses have to deal with two basic constituencies: One is the business, the other is the staff. Of, course, there is some overlap—how can any business question not involve people to some extent, but in most situations you can determine if it is essentially a business issue or a people issue. It's important that you make the distinction because how you approach it will differ accordingly.

For the boss, people issues usually means dealing with the people who report to you. Here are some "people issue" words: support, encourage, coach, teach, protect, punish, listen, sympathize, praise, criticize constructively, help, guide, and lead. Note that missing from the list is "manage." A lot of management problems stem from the word itself; new managers believe—not unreasonably—that their job is to manage the staff, which is almost the last thing the staff want or need.

What does need require managing, however, is the business. Included in this category are such things as systems, budgets, forecasts, expenses, equipment, procedures, customer relationships, goods and services. All these things can be managed in the conventional sense.

Here are some "business" words: organize, analyze, outsource, re-tool, revise, systematize, control, streamline, and manage.

You can't organize people; they have to organize themselves, but you can organize a system or a process. Conversely, it's impossible to "encourage" a system. It's easy to think you can control the people, but you never really can. You can control a system, and then require that people work within the system.

The distinction between managing the business and leading the people is fundamental to a boss's understanding of her job, and the quicker she realizes this the less misery she and her staff will have to endure.

This leads to a final point, which is that the skills needed to manage a business and lead the people are very different. You can have a boss who is a great motivator, but who is presiding over an infrastructure that is falling apart because he does not want to address it. This will catch up with him. On the other hand, you can have a boss who runs a carefully managed business, but is uninspiring to his colleagues, and does not provide them with the leadership they need. This will in time prove equally detrimental to the boss's career. To be an outstanding boss means performing each function well; this is rare. It is the main reason why there are so many bad bosses, and it is also why those who excel at both functions usually rise to the highest levels in their company.

54

VISION VERSUS REALITY

Not exactly as you planned it

Because in business so many carefully made plans go awry, the title of this chapter might serve as a subtitle for the book. Part of your job—a large part—will be devoted to analyzing your operation and thinking of ways to make it better. We've seen how it's important not to expect to make huge strides forward and how important it is to create effectiveness over efficiency so that you don't get too wrapped up in internal processes for their own sake.

However, there will be times when reorganization appears inevitable, and notwithstanding all the diligent incremental advances you've made, occasionally you do have to take a big step and now it's time. To veteran office workers in corporations across America, "reorganization" is a word that makes spirits sag. The cozy familiarity of the status quo to which they've learned to acclimatize will now be destroyed, and they will end up who knows where, and reporting to who knows whom.

Reorganizations are not necessarily bad. Operations do get stale, processes can be improved, people advance at different speeds, and the alert boss keeps a sharp eye on all this, and like a good sailboat captain, she will decide it's time to tack and change course.

Bad reorganizations are often done not because they are needed, but because management is desperately looking for a way to turn things around. Such reorganizations are undertaken in the hope that somehow the reorganization will cause problems to evaporate. This is bad logic. If there is a problem, it should be addressed and fixed, not hidden behind the smoke screen of reorganization.

Let's suppose that the reorganization you are planning is a positive move, and is a genuine attempt on your part to improve things. If it's drastic enough, it will consume your thoughts.

After agonizing about the details of the reorganization, you will play it out in your mind, go over how you will announce it to the individuals most affected and then the whole operation. You will anticipate various reactions, objections, support, pleasure and disgust. You might even make contingency plans for someone who gets so upset that he wants to leave.

That done and the plan finalized, you begin the implementation process that you've been visualizing for weeks. Be prepared for surprises. Kathy, who you thought would love it, is unhappy. Dave, who you were terrified might quit, merely shrugs and says it sounds fine. And as more reactions ripple back, you realize that the plan and the responses that you visualized have taken on a wholly different form from what you expected. You might be lucky; staff reaction may not be completely counter to your expectations, but the results will almost certainly be different in real life from your dreams.

Don't get too upset or disenchanted. This is how the workplace is. You might not like to face it, but you do not have a perfect office with perfectly predictable colleagues. Nor does anyone else. So when it comes time for that big reorganization, consider it, do it, and then expect to be surprised.

55

PERFORMANCE REVIEWS

Don't avoid them or devalue them

For many managers in corporate America, even though things may be going well, the numbers looking good and the horizon appears unclouded, the thought of impending performance reviews can dampen any spirits. In fact, I'm sure many managers would rather spend an hour doing almost anything than conduct an appraisal. That is why, whatever corporate policy says, they are often not done.

But they are important, and they need not be so awful. The main reason annual appraisals are viewed with such fear by managers is that they have failed to perform "rolling" appraisals throughout the year. This is a lot easier said than done. It doesn't mean you have to hold formal review sessions all through the year—although for some people who are being monitored with a view to being dismissed, it can be a necessity. It means that if someone does something bad, or needs correction, action should be taken at once, and documentation created, if appropriate. By doing this, lots of benefits accrue.

First, the employee knows immediately and unambiguously that something was not right. He doesn't have to wait six month to be surprised, or even stunned, by news of his past errors that he might have forgotten about. He can learn from his mistake, and hopefully reduce the chance of repeating it. It's important that you assume the role of coach immediately after the role of schoolmaster: Point out how he can correct it, and work with him to see he does.

And it's also good for the boss to address it right away so that it doesn't fester in the boss's mind. One of the worst things you can do in an appraisal is to save up a complaint till review time and then blast the unsuspecting employee. Fix it quickly, and everyone is a lot happier. This way, when review time comes, you can look at progress made since the infraction and a potentially bad experience can be made into a positive one.

Though less crucial, the same is true for praise. Praise, like criticism, is best applied quickly at the time it was earned. To wait four months before saying in the awkward setting of an appraisal, "Nice work on the Consolidated account back in June," is like giving someone a stale beer.

An appraisal should also take into account the various challenges faced by the individual throughout the year. If someone worked hard and successfully to bring in new clients only to lose a big customer because of a corporate merger, be sure to acknowledge this circumstance, and don't penalize the person for losing the revenue.

If you admonish or compliment as things happen and then take time to note their personal file, you will find that the yearly appraisal process becomes almost a non-event. The employee knows exactly how she is doing because you tell her on a regular basis, and she won't walk out of the annual session with the huge burden of having to correct a problem she only just realized she had. It's positive leadership, and will make everyone much happier.

A final comment: Make sure that your expectations are clear enough so that performance can be benchmarked against them.

This was addressed in Chapter 4, but it is worth repeating here. Unclear expectations are always bad, but during the appraisal process, clarity is critical.

56

PEOPLE

They can learn but they can't change

It all comes down, you will hear it said, to people. What is really meant is that if you have good people, you'll be fine, and if you don't, you will probably not. I agree that if you have great people, however terrible a manager you are, it is almost impossible to make them fail. If you don't have great people, no amount of brilliant management or leadership will make them great.

Several years ago, my former company spent a lot of money—millions of dollars—on a program to enhance the sales abilities of its employees. The sales course consisted of an initial five days, followed up by three more days several months later. This particular program divided humans into four basic personality types: Driver, Analytical, Expressive and Amiable. (There are other programs that categorize character in a similar manner, but give them different labels.)

There was also a spatial element in the theory, which represented these characteristics in a grid with four quadrants. The top two from left to right were Analytical and Driver, and the bottom two were Amiable and Expressive.

Your precise character was a function of exactly where on the grid your profiling put you. For example, you could be a Driver with Expressive characteristics, which would mean your "spot" was in the Driver quadrant but towards the Expressive quadrant.

The quadrants diagonally opposed were deemed to be opposite in nature so that it was unlikely a Driver would have many Amiable tendencies, or an Analytical to have Expressive tendencies. Having found our position, we learned that one of the secrets to being a good sales person was to spot the personality profile of the person you were selling to and adapt yourself to that style.

So if you were an Expressive person, but were having to deal with a potential customer you deemed to be Analytical, you had to take a deep breath and relate to her in analytical terms: details, numbers, words, information, and curb your natural impulse to gloss things over. In this way you would strike a chord and make the sale.

It was all very interesting, although they took eight days to do what could have taken at most four. The very best salespeople, we learned, were those whose character hovered at some midpoint between the quadrants, enabling them to "see in" to the other quadrants, or else were so gifted at adapting that they could moderate their own behavior to react to the circumstances.

Over the course of several years, hundreds of employees were sent away from this course with the insight to be better salesmen. But nothing really changed. The great salespeople continued to be great, only now they had a description given to what they had previously been doing instinctively. The poor salespeople continued to be poor, and the mediocre were still mediocre; they just all now knew why they were poor or mediocre—if they cared to admit it.

"Oh yes," said the Amiables, "I guess I have to be a bit tougher and get into the details a little more." "Hmm!" said the Drivers, "I suppose I should try to be a bit more sensitive," and so on. But they couldn't do it. Just because people know what they need to do, it doesn't mean they know how to do it or are able to do it. It means that the best people have good habits, the bad people have bad habits and the average people have a bit of both; they won't change, and they can't change.

Pick up the sports section of the newspaper during the summer and look at the baseball batting averages. A very good hitter has a .300 or better average. Look how many (or how few) there are. Moreover, their averages tend to remain the same during their professional lifetime. They are referred to-labeled-as a ".240 hitter" or a ".265" hitter. The .200 hitter would love to be better, everyone would love them to be better, but they are what they are, and eventually no one gets too upset because they can't hit .346, they just pay them less or cut them.

Yet, in the corporate world, if someone is the equivalent of a .200 hitter, it's a problem that people often try to change. "Send her on a course," "Bring in the consultants," but just as you can't make a .200 hitter a .300 hitter, you can't make these workers much better. Why should everyone be deemed suitable to do well in corporate America? We don't deem every professional baseball player to be capable of hitting .300.

What you *are* able to do is teach people techniques, such as how to give better presentations, or how to improve their writing skills, or even the use of body language when talking to employees. By doing this you are giving them better tools to do their job, just as you would give them better computers or a better telephone system. But although you can teach people, it's extremely hard to change them. Many operations confuse these very different goals, and are consequently mystified and annoyed when an expensive "people-changing initiative" proves mostly ineffective.

57

A SPORTS LESSON

Some insights from professional sports

The contribution of professional sports to the business world has primarily been its terminology, especially that of baseball: to "strike out," "throw someone a curve," hit a "home run," and so on. Because they are used so often, these phrases have become clichés, but they are still graphic. Indeed, a baseball analogy is used in the previous chapter.

Professional sports organizations often struggle financially, partly as a result of emotional decisions overriding business realities. However, it should be remembered that in professional sports the very best performers in the country are constantly pitted against each other. This extreme level of competition, where success is very publicly measured with relentless precision, produces some interesting operational principles. Here are some of them.

(1) In general there is little room for sentiment in professional sports. A player is either worth their place or they are released. Maybe a heroic veteran will get some special consideration, but not for too long. And if you are not a hero and not performing, you will be very quickly gone. This might be too heartless for corporate life, where a

more generous approach is possible, but as a basic principle is worth bearing in mind.

(2) They are always looking to improve the team by nurturing from within the system or by bringing in fresh blood, if appropriate. However good a season the team may have had, next year is a new story, and they are always making plans for the future.

(3) They only allow players to perform at the highest level when they are ready. They tend not to give under qualified people tasks that are beyond them.

(4) They are always looking to revitalize their image, for example, by redesigning uniforms.

(5) They look to improve the environment of the fans (their customers) by building new stadiums and arenas, hoping this will ultimately lead to increased revenue.

(6) They know that the more money you are prepared to pay in salaries, the better will be the players that you'll attract. The weakest teams invariably invest the least in salaries.

(7) They have many specialized coaches, to make sure that the players get the highest level of continual instruction. This is in spite of the fact that they already hire the most talented performers.

(8) They fully recognize that just because someone was a great player does not mean he will be a great coach or manager. In fact, the reverse is often the case. They do not move star performers into roles they are not suited for.

All of these points have some relevance for business and especially for the manager; there is more to be learned than just some familiar metaphors.

"Productivity is up nine per cent since I made everyone a vice-president."

58

PROMOTIONS

Titles are an important part of corporate life

Assistant vice president, vice president, senior vice president, executive vice president, chief operating officer, president. Titles are an essential lubricant of the American corporate machine. Occasionally, you will hear of a company that has banished titles and tried to flatten out the hierarchical structure, but these are few. For the most part, corporate America still bestows lots of titles as the only visible badge of success.

The importance of titles is often debated. "Just give me the money, I don't care what you call me," is something you will occasionally hear. However, unless you work in an environment where everyone is very highly compensated, there will not be enough money to make everyone happy enough to ignore titles. So, like most of corporate America, you will be asked to distribute a total salary budget increase of maybe three to five percent while your staff has worked hard to increase profits by fifteen percent.

For the boss, titles are important because they are "in kind" rewards that you have at your disposal to hand out: They are currency. In addition, titles are important because most people feel them to be important. Whatever you personally may think of titles, it is certain that the people reporting to you view them as very important, and therefore you should not underestimate them. Having already received a nice title, you might not be quite so concerned, but remember most of your employees aspire to that title.

In the performance reviews I conducted, a discussion of titles was invariably involved, mostly along the lines of, "When will I be considered for promotion to assistant vice president, or vice president." Their unspoken (but sometimes not!) belief was that they felt themselves to be ready for that title right now.

As a general rule, the larger the organization, the more that titles are critical in the minds of the staff. If no one really knows your salary, titles are the only way that the world can measure status and achievement. In a small operation, positive feedback from senior management is easy to come by: "Hey Mary, nice job on the Smith Account!" shouts out the boss as he passes Mary's office. In a huge organization, the big boss is shielded from Mary by layers of management, so that such instant praise and recognition (which is often the most rewarding) is rare. This means that in a big company, for Mary to have succeeded in the eyes of her colleagues, her friends and her family, she needs a title. You are viewed as the proprietor of the title store: Don't take the responsibility lightly.

59

IS IT FOR YOU?

Is being a boss what you really want?

In this book, you will have seen how being a boss involves confronting and handling an array of issues in the workplace. A former boss told me that one day someone would come into my office and tell me something that would completely stun me. He was correct. But whether it's a bizarre situation or one of the more routine problems of the workplace, the boss is required and expected to talk clearly and candidly to the staff involved and to take action.

By definition, a boss is not always the bearer of good news. Good news tends to deal with itself and gets passed on easily. Bad news needs a lot more effort and is much harder to handle. As suggested through the book, it is difficult to be in this position. If doing the things I have described does not appeal, you should seriously question whether being boss is the best thing for you and everyone else. The mistake is often made in promoting someone to supervisor for merely traditional reasons: he was "due;" he was the "obvious" choice; he had been doing well in one role so he was being rewarded with another.

Being promoted to boss and supervising people is still the dominant form of recognition in corporate America. As a result, every year thousands of successful employees are plucked from doing what they do well and set to work at something very different. If you feel that it is not for you, try to have the courage to admit it to yourself and your company. Being open about this might still be a gamble, but many organizations will be grateful for this honesty and work to ensure you continue to do what you do best and enjoy, with suitable recognition.

This is a good time to point out that even the very best bosses never get it right the whole time, and neither will you. Regardless of how deeply you may think through a particular problem, you can still arrive at a wrong answer or a solution that is ineffective. Virtually none of the conclusions in this book were arrived at intuitively: They were all learned on the job, sometimes painfully. You should also be reassured by the knowledge that the more time you spend being the boss, the better you get at it.

No boss relishes every aspect of what they do; being a good manager doesn't make it easy or enjoyable to tell someone they are not getting promoted or they are not getting a raise. Having said all that, I'll repeat what I said in the introduction: Leading a committed group of people in a successful business enterprise is immensely satisfying.

EPILOGUE

There are lots of ways that corporate America can make you upset. You get passed over for a deserved promotion, you are underpaid, your health care coverage is constantly being changed, your retirement plan is redesigned for the worse, you miss out on the good assignments, you get a tiny workspace, you have poor equipment, you get stuck with colleagues you don't like; all these things are aggravating, but short of firing you, the very worst thing a company can do is give you a terrible boss.

If you are the boss, you have it in your power to greatly reduce some of this potential for suffering, and turn what can be a dreaded experience into one that is tolerable and sometimes actually enjoyable. Do not underestimate the positive or negative impact you can have. It's not easy to be a good boss; it's hard work that demands constant attention. When I first became a boss, I would have found a book like this very helpful; I hope this one helps you.

BVG